MEXICO IN TRANSITION
IMPLICATIONS FOR U.S. POLICY

Essays from Both Sides of the Border

Susan Kaufman Purcell, Editor

Council on Foreign Relations
New York

COUNCIL ON FOREIGN RELATIONS BOOKS

The Council on Foreign Relations, Inc., is a nonprofit and nonpartisan organization devoted to promoting improved understanding of international affairs through the free exchange of ideas. The Council does not take any position on questions of foreign policy and has no affiliation with, and receives no funding from, the United States government.

From time to time, books and monographs written by members of the Council's research staff or visiting fellows, or commissioned by the Council, or written by an independent author with critical review contributed by a Council study or working group are published with the designation "Council on Foreign Relations Book." Any book or monograph bearing that designation is, in the judgment of the Committee on Studies of the Council's board of directors, a responsible treatment of a significant international topic worthy of presentation to the public. All statements of fact and expressions of opinion contained in Council books are, however, the sole responsibility of the author.

Library of Congress Cataloging-in-Publication Data

Mexico in transition.
    Bibliography: p.
    1. United States—Relations—Mexico. 2. Mexico—Relations—
United States. 3. Mexico—Economic conditions—1970–
I. Purcell, Susan Kaufman.
II. Title.
E183.8.M6M476   1988   303.4'8273'072   88-10949

ISBN 0-87609-028-5

MEXICO IN TRANSITION

Contents

Foreword

Mexico and the United States are united by geography and divided by history. Our common border, nearly two thousand miles long, once divided empty spaces on the far frontiers of both countries. Today, however, those empty spaces are filling up as Mexico's population skyrockets toward a hundred million and beyond, and as America shifts toward the Sunbelt. Along the border, poverty and opulence, hope and despair, crowd together separated only by the strands of wire fences. On winter nights one can see the bonfires ringed by huddled groups waiting for a chance to dash north across the border—toward Los Angeles, Phoenix, San Antonio and beyond.

But as our countries crowd together, our political institutions continue to pass in the night, as remote and uncommunicative as ever. Part of the problem is our differing institutional systems. Americans take their economic and political institutions from a Protestant parliamentary tradition of decentralized and dispersed decision making. Mexican institutions, in contrast, reflect the authoritarian, centralized heritage of the Spanish Crown and the Catholic Church.

Other differences reflect the unsettling experience with manifest destiny along the border: the struggle for Texas; the Mexican War; an episode of intervention during the Mexican Revolution; and the inevitable frictions arising from the huge and persistent economic differentials that produce both opportunity and nationalistic resentment on the Mexican side.

Our diplomatic and economic relations tend to get tangled up in this complex historical reality. In Mexico City, the American Ambassador is always a celebrity—and often a scapegoat for the accumulated frustrations of the Mexican government and press. In Washington, the Mexican diplomatic mission, inhibited by its sensitivity to American presence in Mexico, has been excessively low key and slow to mobilize its natural Mexican–American constituency in support of Mexican objectives.

At the popular level, television, which does not respect boundaries, is both bringing us closer together and sharpening the perception of differences. American television programming exerts a strong influence in Mexico, while Mexican television, less noticed, is a powerful new cultural presence in most American cities.

Given the lack of mutual understanding, it is hardly surprising that many Mexicans profess a dislike of America even as they proclaim their admiration for Americans. And the opposite is true as well: most Americans perceive individual Mexicans as energetic, hard working, family oriented people, whose full potential is held in check by a corrupt and incompetent government.

Many of us who live along the border sense that the old, lackadaisical, myth-ridden approach to our relations cannot continue too much longer. The problems continue to multiply. The episodic disputes over energy issues that took place during the 1970s have given way to a prolonged debt crisis. Occasional trade disputes have pyramided into a more general conflict over loss of American jobs and claims that the *maquila* industries, so vital to the border economy, are undermining the strength of the American labor movement. Unattended and unresolved drug trafficking issues also prompt an increasingly impatient Congress to move even more toward retaliatory measures.

The challenge for both our countries is to work together toward a coherent, generally understood and accepted set of bilateral policies grounded in a realistic understanding of the possibilities—and limitations—imposed by historical and cultural realities. Precisely because we are so close—and so interdependent—the task cannot be left to a few diplomats in Washington and Mexico City. A successful, enduring relation must be built on a broad base of communication, understanding and cultural and institutional ties. This book of essays, and the study groups that preceded it, are a beginning that should be repeated many times in both countries.

Bruce Babbitt

April 1988

Preface

Mexico has been experiencing important economic, political and social changes during the six years since the onset of the debt crisis. Some are the result of government policies. Others are the consequence of the abrupt end of two decades of nearly continuous economic growth that preceded the crisis. Some seem fairly easy to manage and assimilate. Others appear to be potentially threatening to Mexico's future peace and prosperity.

Despite an impressive increase in media coverage of developments in Mexico since August 1982, however, Americans remain uncertain as to how to evaluate events south of the 2,000-mile shared border. This is not only because of differences in our histories, cultures, wealth and power. It also relates to the fact that there is no consensus, both within each of our two countries and between them, regarding the implications of the changed situation for Mexico and for its relationship with the United States.

This brief volume is an attempt to help Americans better understand the challenges facing Mexico today, as well as the widely diverging assessments of what is being done and still remains to be done to meet them. In the process, it addresses directly and indirectly the prospects for political unrest, serious instability, breakdown or even a second revolution in Mexico, questions that are perhaps uppermost in the minds of Americans as they try to form their own opinions regarding what the United States can or should do to help its neighbor.

Six of the eleven authors are Mexican and five are from the United States. They include politicians, diplomats, private sector representatives and professors. All have written broad-brushed interpretive essays for a principally non-Mexican and non-expert audience. Sometimes the views and arguments in the different essays reinforce each other. At other times, they are strikingly contradictory. As a result, the volume leads the reader to no obvious or easy conclusions. Instead, it illustrates the persistence of cross-cultural misperceptions between Mexico and the United States and sheds light on the difficulties of managing the bilateral relationship.

Most of the essays in this volume originated as oral presentations to the members of a Council on Foreign Relations study group on Mexico, organized and directed by Susan Kaufman Purcell and chaired by former Arizona governor Bruce Babbitt. Two of the contributions, however, were first delivered to the members of a subsequently organized study group on Mexico and Central America, held in Los Angeles for West Coast members of the Council on Foreign Relations.

Organization of this Book

This book is divided into four parts. The first presents an American and a Mexican overview of the Mexican government's response to the economic and political challenges facing the country since the onset of the debt crisis. The lead essay by Susan Kaufman Purcell, "Mexico in Transition," presents an essentially positive evaluation of President de la Madrid's efforts to deal with the crisis. Jorge G. Castañeda is less enthusiastic. In "The Choice Facing Mexico," he questions the basic rationale for the economic austerity programs and efforts to liberalize the economy. He also asks whether most Mexicans want democracy as it is understood in the United States.

The second section of the book deals with the politics of key Mexican interest groups. In "The Changing Role of the Private Sector," Luis Rubio explains why business-government relations have grown more conflictual over time and why the private sector is divided over President de la Madrid's economic policies. "The Impact of the Economic Crisis on the Mexican Political System," by Soledad Loaeza, analyses why right-of-center parties and interest groups have been strengthened by the crisis. David Ronfeldt then examines the changing role of the Mexican military and the transformation of Mexico's political elite in "Questions and Cautions About Mexico's Future."

In a special section on immigration, included because of the new situation facing Mexico and the United States in the aftermath of the recent passage of the Simpson/Rodino legislation, Jorge Bustamante criticizes unilateral decisionmaking by the United States in his essay, "U.S. Immigration Reform: A Mexican Perspective." In contrast, Manuel García y Griego, an American who teaches and lives in Mexico, points out in "A Bilateral Approach to Migration?" that a bilateral approach to the control of undocumented migration from Mexico is difficult and possibly even undesirable. Finally, in "The New Immigration Law and Mexico," Doris Meissner explains what the U.S. and Mexico now must do to ensure the smooth and equitable implementation of the Simpson/Rodino law.

The last section of the book deals with the overall U.S.–Mexican relationship. "On the Formulation of U.S. Policy toward Mexico," José Juan de Olloqui criticizes the U.S. for generally ignoring Mexico and argues for a comprehensive policy that would include U.S. efforts to strengthen Mexico's economy while avoiding interference in Mexico's internal politics. Adolfo Aguilar Zinser warns that continued U.S. efforts to find solutions for Mexico's problems that primarily serve U.S. interests will increase bilateral conflict and exacerbate political struggles within Mexico. And in "U.S.–Mexican Relations: Time for a Change," Donald Lyman criticizes crisis decisionmaking and advises the U.S. to work with Mexico toward resolving a few specific, but important, problems.

Acknowledgments

This collection of essays by Mexicans and Americans benefited from the contributions of a number of people. I owe a very special vote of thanks to former governor Bruce Babbitt of Arizona, who was a dynamic and intellectually provocative chairman of the East Coast Study Group on Mexico, sponsored by the Council on Foreign Relations. The comments by the members of this Study Group, as well as those of the West Coast Study Group on Mexico, also sponsored by the Council, in cooperation with UCLA's Center for International and Strategic Affairs and its director, Michael Intriligator, were invaluable. I am very grateful to my former assistant, Patricia Ravalgi, for helping to organize and coordinate the study groups and for working with the authors in the early stages of this project. Ana Lopez did outstanding work in editing the original version of the manuscript. Dore Hollander's excellent editing of the final versions of the essays is also greatly appreciated. I wish to thank my current assistant, Stephanie Golob, for her valuable editorial suggestions, for preparing the Chronology and for her efforts in putting the volume into its completed form. Ambassador William Luers and Ambassador Diego Asencio provided thoughtful comments and critiques for revision of the essays prior to their publication. David Kellogg and Jeremy Brenner of the Council on Foreign Relations' publication office also offered useful advice.

Both this publication and the study groups that gave it shape were funded by grants to the Latin American Project of the Council on Foreign Relations from The Tinker Foundation, The Andrew W. Mellon Foundation, The Ford Foundation and by the personal generosity of Richard Mallery and Jerry Nelson of Arizona.

Susan Kaufman Purcell

April 1988

Part I
Overview

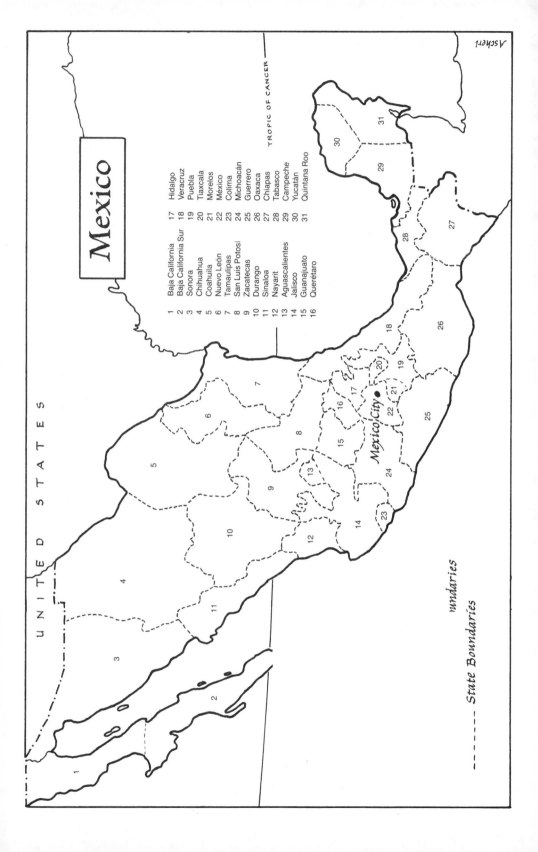

Mexico

1	Baja California	17	Hidalgo
2	Baja California Sur	18	Veracruz
3	Sonora	19	Puebla
4	Chihuahua	20	Tlaxcala
5	Coahuila	21	Morelos
6	Nuevo León	22	México
7	Tamaulipas	23	Colima
8	San Luis Potosí	24	Michoacán
9	Zacatecas	25	Guerrero
10	Durango	26	Oaxaca
11	Sinaloa	27	Chiapas
12	Nayarit	28	Tabasco
13	Aguascalientes	29	Campeche
14	Jalisco	30	Yucatán
15	Guanajuato	31	Quintana Roo
16	Querétaro		

UNITED STATES

TROPIC OF CANCER

Mexico City

----- State Boundaries

Ascheri

Mexico in Transition

Susan Kaufman Purcell

Mexico's political stability has generally coincided with long periods of sustained economic growth. Since the onset of the debt crisis in August 1982, economic growth has proved elusive. Political tensions have increased as a result. To resolve both problems, Mexico's leaders have been trying to restructure the economy. Their goal is to make the economic system more competitive internationally by reducing protectionism and decreasing the role of the state in the economy. Their efforts at economic liberalization have reinforced long-standing demands for democratization of the political system. The United States has supported and encouraged both kinds of liberalization. It should and will continue to do so, although heavy-handed pressure for political change will exacerbate bilateral conflicts.

UNTIL THE ONSET OF the debt crisis in August 1982, Mexico was considered a Latin American "success story." For decades it had a stable government under civilian control, in marked contrast to most of Latin America. It also had enjoyed continuous and often spectacular rates of economic growth, averaging between six and eight percent during the 1950s and 1960s. There was, however, a dark side to these achievements. The political system was stable, but not democratic. It was dominated by the Partido Revolucionario Institucional (PRI), which usually won elections but resorted to electoral fraud when it did not. Furthermore, the system was highly corrupt. And although the economy grew rapidly, so did the gap between the rich and the poor. By the 1980s, Mexico's distribution of resources was one of the most highly skewed in the hemisphere.

But as long as the system "worked," people on both sides of the U.S.–Mexican border were willing to overlook its failures. This changed after August 1982, however, when Mexicans and Americans alike began to question whether political stability could be maintained without high levels of economic growth. Underlying the question was the sense that resources generated by a growing economy had been used to paper over problems rather than resolve them. It was unclear how the system would cope with the growing demands being

3

made upon it, once the "squeaking wheels" could no longer be greased.

The crisis also produced pressures for political and economic liberalization. The large role that the state had played in Mexico's economy, as well as the centralization of political power within the PRI, were seen as having contributed to the economic crisis. It seemed logical, therefore, to seek solutions to Mexico's problems by moving away from the political and economic status quo.

The loss of confidence in Mexico's economic and political systems was reinforced by changes in the international environment. By the early 1980s, the world's love affair with statist development strategies was winding down. Socialism now seemed better at producing bureaucracy than economic growth. The heretofore unfashionable private sector was increasingly viewed as the alternative engine necessary to lead Third World countries to prosperity.

The new push for economic liberalization was paralleled by a growing enthusiasm for democracy. Of all the developing areas, Latin America had made the most progress in this respect. By the 1980s, both Brazil and Argentina had replaced military leaders with civilians. Even the often denigrated "banana republics" of Central America were now governed by democratically-elected presidents.

In contrast, Mexico seemed to be stagnating politically. When most of Latin America had been governed by authoritarian military regimes, Mexico's civilian one-party dominant system looked relatively good. In the context of an overwhelmingly democratic hemisphere, however, Mexico's political system appeared considerably less attractive.

The economic crisis, together with the changed economic and political environment, sparked an intense debate within Mexico over the kinds of policies Mexico should adopt to meet its new challenges. Some important changes have already been implemented. In some areas, however, there is more talk than action. Two basic questions remain unanswered: Can the Mexican government succeed in restoring economic growth while maintaining political stability? And is there a constructive role that the United States can play during this difficult period?

I

Because the economic crisis caused people to question prospects for continued political stability, the government decided to give top priority to restoring economic growth. Economic revival would dampen economic and political discontent, thereby allowing the government to postpone dealing with the riskier and more contentious issue of political reform.

The strategy adopted by President Miguel de la Madrid for reviving Mexico's economy was economic liberalization. In essence, this implied reducing the state's economic role, reducing or eliminating import barriers and obstacles to foreign investment, and encouraging a more dynamic private sector.

The commitment to economic liberalization has several explanations. Perhaps most important is the obvious lack of resources to sustain import-substitution–industrialization, the expensive state-led development strategy that Mexico and other Latin American countries had adopted after World War II. Henceforth, private capital, both domestic and foreign, would have to play a greater role in generating growth. Second, the economic crisis provided critics of a state-led development strategy with the political space to press for a different approach. The proponents of economic liberalization were also strengthened by change in the international economic environment, which now favored a development strategy that focused on private investment and a smaller state role in the economy. Finally, Mexico's foreign debt, which totaled nearly $90 billion by mid-1982, made the government dependent on financial institutions such as the International Monetary Fund and the World Bank. These organizations, together with the private commercial banks to which Mexico also owed substantial funds, strongly urged the adoption of policies to reduce state spending and open up the Mexican economy.

Perhaps the most important symbol of the government's commitment to economic liberalization was its decision to join the General Agreement on Tariffs and Trade (GATT). The de la Madrid administration also tried to open the economy by lowering tariffs, eliminating licenses for a large number of goods, and providing greater incentives to export. State spending has been reduced in part by dismissing public-sector employees and selling or closing unprofitable state-owned enterprises. Although the government has refused to change Mexico's foreign investment law, which limits foreign ownership to 49 percent in most enterprises, it has nevertheless adopted a more flexible approach. For example, the government allowed IBM to exercise 100 percent ownership. Government officials have also substituted more welcoming rhetoric for what, in the past, was often a hostile attitude toward foreign investment. Finally, the government has reduced or eliminated subsidies in many sectors and continues to promote economic decentralization.

In terms of the policies that prevailed before 1982, these steps represent a significant change in both attitude and behavior on the part of the government. Nevertheless, Mexico's commitment to economic liberalization has been less than clear-cut. Frequently, the government appears to take one step backward for every two steps forward. It dismisses some government employees, but then rehires them elsewhere. It removes import licenses for domestic industries that do not need protection, but keeps them for other industries that do, or uses licenses to punish opponents of government policies. It decreases government spending one year, only to increase it the next, usually in response to political pressures.

These mixed signals have several explanations. Economic liberalization adversely affects those who profit from a large economic role for the state. In Mexico, the "statists" are found mainly in ministries or agencies that own or control public companies, including the Ministry of National Patrimony and Industry, Petróleos Mexicanos (PEMEX)—the government-owned petroleum industry, Teléfonos de México, and the Federal Electricity Commission. Their presence is strong in the Federation of Government Employees (FSTSE), which dominates the labor sector of the PRI.

Until the 1970s, the enormous power of the state was offset in part by a wealthy and powerful private sector. This enabled the government to balance the various interests represented in the dominant party and the state bureaucracy against the interests of the private sector. By playing these interests off against each other, the president could maintain some independence from all organized interests. The power of those who benefited from the strong economic role of the state was offset by the power of those who benefited from the presence of a strong private sector.

Beginning with the presidency of Luis Echeverría Alvarez (1970–1976), however, the balance began to tip toward the statists. Echeverría greatly increased state spending, in part to defuse the discontent and alienation produced by the so-called Tlatelolco Massacre, on which occasion hundreds of students were killed by the military. He also hoped to spur economic growth by virtue of such spending, and thereby satisfy the growing demands being made upon the government. Echeverría's successor, José López Portillo (1976–1982), further undermined the traditional balance by engaging in even more ambitious spending, using the resources generated by the oil boom. When oil prices collapsed in 1981, López Portillo decided to increase Mexico's indebtedness rather than change his development plans, and massive capital flight ensued. The nationalization of the banking system in the last few months of his administration—which he justified as necessary to stop capital flight, but which was motivated more by selfish political reasons—further undermined the private sector.

President de la Madrid's efforts to liberalize the economy are partially aimed at restoring the old equilibrium between the public and private sectors. Economic liberalization, therefore, has two goals. The first is the revival of the Mexican economy. The second, and perhaps no less important, goal is the restoration of the political space that the president needs to maintain Mexico's political stability.

It is far from assured, however, that current efforts to liberalize the economy will go far enough. The problem involves more than just opposition from the statists. Even supporters of a more open economy cannot be certain that it will yield the desired economic results. Industrial countries with strong private sectors and a commitment to free trade are not, after all, currently experiencing impressive economic growth. Given the absence of guarantees that the political risks of economic liberalization will be offset by economic recovery, the de la Madrid administration's less-than-wholehearted commitment to liberalization of the economy appears more understandable. Second, successful economic liberalization implies closer de facto economic integration with the United States. Among Mexicans this prospect stirs up fears of U.S. domination and the loss of Mexico's identity. It also allows the statists to appeal to Mexican nationalism and the always latent anti-Americanism to block the liberalization policies that they consider most damaging to their interests.

Finally, even government officials who today strongly support efforts to liberalize the Mexican economy are, at heart, proponents of a relatively strong Mexican state. Their views have been shaped by a "revolutionary" ideology that considers the private sector antirevolutionary because it opposed the Mexican Revolution of 1910. They also regard businessmen as anti-Mexican because the latter emphasize profits over politics. Most important, however, government officials do not take well to policies that undermine their own political power. Hence, economic liberalization, which implies greater decentralization of economic resources and, by extension, of political power, is desirable only up to a point. That point is probably the reestablishment of the traditional balance between the public and private sectors. Economic liberalization does not imply tipping the scales to the extent that the private sector could seriously block government-sponsored initiatives. What the government is hoping to achieve through its economic liberalization efforts, therefore, is a more dynamic and competitive economy and private sector, as well as a more efficient, legitimate and, hence, stronger state.

II

The efforts to liberalize the Mexican economy have reinforced long-standing demands for democratization. Many Mexicans believe that economic and political liberalization are linked; the economy cannot be decentralized and opened up without corresponding political changes. The immediate beneficiary of these ideas is Mexico's main opposition party, the Partido de Acción Nacional (PAN), which has long advocated a smaller role for the state in the economy, a strong private sector, and honest elections.

Ironically, demands for democratization have also strengthened the bargaining power of the statists within the PRI. Members of the recently organized *corriente democratica,* or "democratic current," however, originally advocated not the democratization of the political system, but the democratization of the official party. By calling for more rank-and-file participation in the selection of President de la Madrid's successor, they had hoped to capitalize on the widespread discontent with the government's economic austerity measures and to nominate one of their own as the PRI's presidential candidate. Once in control of the party, and then of the government, they would have tried to have forced a return to Mexico's traditional, state-led development model. When President de la Madrid succeeded in maintaining control of the nomination process and selected Carlos Salinas de Gortari as the PRI's presidential candidate, Cuauhtemoc Cárdenas decided to run for president on a minor party label. His assured electoral defeat, however, will not mark the end of the conflict over Mexico's future development strategy.

These political considerations help explain the de la Madrid administration's cautious and ambivalent measures to open up the economy. The president knows he is walking a fine line. On the one hand, he needs to liberalize the economy to restore sustained economic growth. On the other hand, he must avoid implementing programs that might strengthen those groups intent on overturning his economic policies, undermining the PRI's dominance, or both.

Demands for political liberalization are nothing new. The PRI has always been somewhat defensive about its control of the Mexican political system. After all, it came to power as the result of a revolution that had as a slogan "Effective suffrage and no reelection." There has been no reelection of a Mexican president since the Revolution, but there has clearly been the reelection of a political party. This has prompted more than one Mexican scholar to describe the Mexican Revolution as having modernized Mexican authoritarianism, transforming it from rule by a traditional dictator to rule by a single party.

The PRI's defensiveness is also related to Mexico's liberal tradition, which dates back to the nineteenth century. Even Porfirio Díaz found it necessary to call repeated elections during his thirty-one-year rule. Since the Revolution and despite the predictable victory of the PRI in presidential and gubernatorial races, elections have been routinely held. Furthermore, the PRI has periodically implemented reforms to make the political system more democratic without ultimately undermining the PRI's status as the "official" party.

The PRI has sometimes been quite imaginative in its reform efforts. In the 1950s it experimented with local primaries instead of imposing candidates chosen by officials in Mexico City. It also tried to end the process whereby representatives of the party's three sectors—the labor, peasant, and "popular" or middle-class sectors—divided nominations among themselves. The results were a disturbing increase in local conflict and a weakening of the party's labor sector. Consequently, these experiments were abandoned and others tried in their stead. In 1962, for example, President Adolfo López Mateos (1958–64) created "party deputies," which increased the representation of opposition parties in the Chamber of Deputies. Reforms introduced by President López Portillo further strengthened opposition parties by making it easier for them to organize and campaign. These reforms mainly benefited the smaller parties at both extremes of the political spectrum. They also enhanced the PRI's ability to divide and rule its competitors. But an overly fragmented opposition is not a credible opposition. President de la Madrid's reforms, therefore, sought to correct this situation by obliging opposition parties to unite in the Chamber of Deputies. At the same time, he ensured the PRI's continued majority status by converting the largest plurality vote (the PRI's) into an automatic majority.

The PRI's concern with its democratic image also explains why the government subsidizes smaller opposition parties. The PRI wants to be the dominant party, not the only party. It has also encouraged opposition parties to run candidates for the presidency for the same reason: running without an opponent undermines the PRI's efforts to portray itself as the most popular party in Mexico's "multiparty" system. Finally, the PRI's concern with its democratic image is behind decisions to allow opposition parties to win elections on the local and state levels, excluding governorships. It also explains efforts to give opposition candidates equal time on television during the 1982 presidential election.

Current demands for democratization have focused mainly on ending electoral fraud. They have been strongest in the north, where the PAN is popular and seemed capable of winning fair elections in a number of recent gubernatorial races. The PAN's newfound strength is clearly linked to Mexico's economic crisis, which many Mexicans blame on the irresponsibility and corruption of de la Madrid's two predecessors, Luis Echeverría Alvarez and, especially, José López Portillo. Discontent with the PRI has produced votes for the PAN.

Evidence of the PRI's resort to electoral fraud in the north indicates that the party has no intention of allowing the PAN to win a governorship, at least for the foreseeable future. PRI officials were apparently divided over this issue. Those who lost had argued that honest elections would not necessarily result in PAN victories or, even if they did, would allow the PRI to survive and would ultimately strengthen the system. Those who won the debate did not want to take the risk. They feared that the deterioration in living standards over the past several years, combined with prospects for continued economic austerity, would produce wholesale voting against the PRI that would take the form of strong support for the PAN. After the first "domino" fell, the PRI's image of invincibility would be destroyed, causing voters in other northern states to follow suit. The more democratically inclined of these PRI hard-liners argued that the party could allow honest elections after the economy had improved. It is not clear, however, what incentive there would be to experiment once the economic crisis was over.

The PRI has, nevertheless, implemented a number of less dramatic reforms, such as choosing better qualified candidates for governorships in the north. In fact, the PRI's candidates were so competitive with those of the PAN that Mexicans described them as being *enpanizados*, or "breaded"—a play on the word *pan*, which in Spanish means bread. The PRI also gave so-called "precandidatos," or contenders for the party's presidential nomination, access to television prior to the decision to choose Carlos Salinas de Gortari as the PRI's candidate.

Further reforms will probably have to wait for the next administration and will most likely involve restoring some of the traditional balance between technocrats and politicians, or at least, giving more power to those technocrats with strong political skills. The last three *sexenios*, or six-year terms, have been dominated by the so-called *técnicos*, highly trained individuals who rose to power through the bureaucracy rather than the party and the electoral system. The rapid ascent of the technocrats paralleled the continuous expansion of the state's role and, with it, the state bureaucracy. It was both a reflection and a cause of the PRI's eroding power and political base. This situation also produced heightened conflict between politicians and technocrats as a result of the passing over of party loyalists for promotion to high office.

The rise of the technocrats caused people to make unfortunate comparisons with the tenure of Porfirio Díaz, when the *científicos,* or adherents of nineteenth-century positivism, tried to develop Mexico by applying scientific principles to government. In failing to recognize the importance of political skills in maintaining stability, the *científicos* helped bring about the Mexican Revolution. Critics of the contemporary "technocracy" warn that the current economic crisis, combined with a failure to restore the old balance between technocrats and politicians, could produce the same unhappy ending.

In addition to strengthening the role of politicians, future reforms will attempt to revitalize the PRI in other ways. One serious problem is the erosion of support for the PRI in urban areas. Traditionally, peasants and organized workers have constituted the most reliable base of support for the party. But as Mexico modernizes, the percentage of peasants in the population continues to decline. Efforts to unionize workers have also not kept pace with the growth of the labor force.

In the next *sexenio,* therefore, the PRI will probably make more of an attempt to create new party organizations among the urban population, such as groups for small businessmen, self-employed individuals, and workers in the service sector. The party will also have to strengthen its penetration of lower-class urban neighborhoods.

A long-standing criticism of the PRI is its imposition of candidates to "represent" areas with which they are unfamiliar. In the future, the party will have to select candidates who not only have local roots but also command significant popular support. In the north, this will mean choosing more lawyers, businessmen, and others from the middle and lower-middle classes. In the south, future candidates will have to have stronger ties with the peasantry. In all cases, however, potential PRI candidates will have to demonstrate they possess considerable political skill. Technocratic expertise will not be sufficient to manage Mexico's increasingly complex political environment.

The selection of candidates who have local bases of support also implies a decrease in Mexico City's control of outlying areas. Such candidates, therefore, constitute a mixed blessing from the point of view of the PRI. On the one hand, they enhance the PRI's legitimacy and support. On the other hand, they threaten the highly centralized political status quo.

Another possible change would involve the establishment of competitive primaries for the selection of PRI candidates. Primaries would help revive interest in the electoral process, which is currently characterized by high rates of abstention, and would also result in the selection of more popular candidates.

At some point, the PRI will probably allow an opposition party to win a governorship. Party officials who favor such a step cite the example of India, where control by opposition parties of some state governments has not undermined the dominant position of the Congress Party. Nonetheless, the PRI will probably not relinquish a governorship until the current economic crisis is resolved, and even then the experiment will not be launched in the wealthy states that border on the United States.

A number of more intractable problems confront the PRI. Organized labor, whose cooperation with the government has hitherto helped ensure political stability and continued PRI dominance, is becoming less cooperative. As economic modernization continues, more skilled and better educated white-collar workers are becoming union members. They are less amenable to government co-optation or control. In addition, the man who deserves a great deal of credit for organized labor's cooperation with the PRI, Fidel Velázquez, is now 87 years old. It is not clear whether his successor will be able to fill his shoes. If political stability is to be maintained in the future, the PRI must devise new ways of relating to a more sophisticated labor movement.

The PRI must also find new ways of dealing with the peasantry. In the past, the government has opted for control, over productivity. It may no longer be able to afford this trade-off. The peasantry's standard of living has improved least in comparison with that of other groups. The extreme poverty that characterizes much of rural Mexico, particularly the south, is allowing left-wing opposition parties to make some headway there. Discontent is exacerbated by the impact of the conflict in Central America. Refugees in numbers estimated to range between several hundred thousand and a million are adding to the burden of already poor state governments in the south and are aggravating high levels of unemployment and underemployment.

Increasing the pace of economic growth in rural Mexico would help alleviate these problems. In the agricultural sector, the *ejido* or collective farm, which allows the government to control the peasantry while providing it with some benefits, is very inefficient. Productivity could be increased by giving *ejidatarios* more control over their land. The

López Portillo administration passed a constitutional amendment that allowed *ejidatarios* to join with private producers to buy machinery and the like. Such reforms should be expanded. Finally, if peasants had more say in the selection of their leaders, their morale and loyalty would improve.

This discussion of possible and probable future reforms suggests that economic liberalization in Mexico is compatible with limited political liberalization. Mexico does not have to become a two-party or multiparty democracy in order to reduce the economic role of the state and liberalize the economy. Instead, it can opt to make its one-party dominant system more representative of changing social and economic structures and more responsive to the needs of its people. To some extent, this process has already begun under President de la Madrid. The danger lies in the possibility that future leaders may overestimate the drawbacks of continued political reform and underestimate its benefits. Should that be the case, Mexico's political system will become increasingly rigid and incapable of dealing successfully with the political and economic challenges that it undoubtedly will face.

III

The economic crisis of the early 1980s has also had repercussions in the area of foreign policy. During the period immediately preceding the de facto default of August 1982, Mexico had been playing an uncharacteristically active international role. In part, this was the result of the oil boom of the 1970s, which provided Mexico with both the status and the resources to pursue an active foreign policy. Moreover, the discovery of oil in Mexico coincided with the period of détente in U.S.–Soviet relations. As concern over the East–West conflict was replaced by an emphasis on North–South issues, advanced developing countries, such as Mexico, gained "political space" in which to operate internationally. The decline in U.S. prestige and authority in the aftermath of Vietnam and Watergate also helped Mexico's quest for an expanded international role.

Central America was one area where Mexican involvement increased. Despite Mexico's supposed support for the principles of self-determination and nonintervention, President López Portillo withdrew recognition from Anastasio Somoza's regime in Nicaragua and joined with other Latin American countries in helping the Sandinistas to overthrow him. When Somoza fled in 1979, López Portillo offered the Sandinistas the use of a Mexican government plane to fly them to Managua. Two years later, Mexico joined with France in issuing a declaration that called the Salvadoran guerrillas "a representative political force." López Portillo also laid the groundwork for Mexico's subsequent leadership role in the Contadora peace process.

By the time Miguel de la Madrid assumed the presidency, however, the conditions that had encouraged Mexico's international activism had begun to change. Détente had collapsed and Ronald Reagan's election to the U.S. presidency restored East–West concerns to prominence on the U.S. foreign policy agenda. Meanwhile, petroleum prices plummeted, depriving Mexico of the resources and influence that had allowed it to pursue a more active foreign policy.

Things also began to change in Central America. The Sandinistas, although continuing to profess nonalignment, had drawn closer to Cuba and the Soviet Union. Central America also became a domestic political issue for Mexico, as tens of thousands of refugees poured across its southern border. With the onset of the debt crisis, the substantial economic aid that Mexico had been giving to the Sandinistas also began to generate opposition, particularly among businessmen and the military, who grew increasingly concerned with the Sandinistas' move to the left. Finally, the debt crisis required Mexico to work more closely with the United States. Many Mexicans began to argue that it was not in Mexico's interest to alienate the Reagan administration by being too supportive of the Sandinistas and working against the policies of the United States within the Contadora process.

The changing reality and growing dissension within Mexico produced a subtle shift in Mexico's Central American policy during the de la Madrid administration. With the election of Napoleón Duarte to the presidency of El Salvador in 1984, Mexico downplayed its support for the Salvadoran guerrillas—it sent its foreign minister to Duarte's inauguration—and also tried to play a more balanced role within the Contadora Group, which sought a negotiated solution to the Central American conflict.

Until the Iran-contra scandal became public, Mexican interest in and involvement with Central America had been slowly declining. Mexicans were far more concerned with their economic crisis and its potential political implications. They seemed to have resigned themselves either to a continuing stalemate in Central America or to the inevitability of a U.S. invasion. In either case, they saw little they could do.

The scandal, however, revived Mexican interest in Central America. The possibility that the U.S. Congress would terminate economic and military aid to the Nicaraguan rebels refocused attention on a negotiated settlement of the conflict. Since Mexico had always opposed U.S. funding of the contras and had advocated a negotiated settlement, the scandal had the immediate effect of reducing U.S.–Mexican tensions over Central America. The subsequent signing by the five Central American presidents of President Oscar Arias' peace plan allowed conflict between the United States and Mexico over Central America to remain lower. This situation could, of course, prove temporary, depending on the future behavior of both the Sandinistas and the United States. In the meantime, the peace process is serving to deflect attention away from Central America as an area of bilateral conflict. At the same time, a number of other problems between the United States and Mexico are creating potential problems for the bilateral relationship in general.

U.S.–Mexican relations have always been difficult to manage. Part of the problem is the asymmetry of power between the two countries. Mexico has not loomed as large for the United States as the United States has loomed for Mexico. And yet, relations between the two countries are rarely as good or as bad as they appear. This is because the health of the bilateral relationship tends to be measured by examining relations at the level of the national governments. Most bilateral ties, however, involve lower levels of government in both countries and a multitude of private relationships on both sides of the border. These are more routine in nature and less subject to the extreme fluctuations that characterize the more public contacts between the two national governments.

Since the onset of the debt crisis, relations between the two national governments have assumed greater importance in the overall relationship. The new situation has prompted rethinking within the U.S. Government regarding the kind of policy that the United States should adopt toward Mexico during its time of troubles.

The goal of U.S. policy has been and continues to be a stable and prosperous Mexico. This is also what Mexico wishes for itself. However, the two governments disagree over what, if anything, the United States should do to help bring about these shared goals. The Mexicans would like the United States to confine its activities to providing debt relief and opening markets for Mexican exports, leaving Mexico to solve its problems as it sees fit. The United States, in contrast, is reluctant to play such a passive role. It also doubts whether the kind of no-strings-attached help that Mexico would like is politically feasible on the domestic front or even desirable from the standpoint of achieving U.S. goals in Mexico. The debt crisis has made many more U.S. citizens aware of Mexico and the negative impact that continued economic problems could have, first on Mexico and then on the United States.

In the area of economics, the United States strongly supports the liberalization and privatization of the Mexican economy so as to stimulate sustained economic growth. Hence, it has worked with the International Monetary Fund and the World Bank to urge reforms on Mexico. Because the United States has not acted unilaterally in the economic arena, and because the changes it favors are generally congruent with the policies of the de la Madrid administration, U.S. economic policy toward Mexico has not generated much conflict between the two countries.

Political pressures, however, are another matter. The U.S. Government has refrained from criticizing the Mexican political system or otherwise undermining the PRI. It recognizes that political pressures from Washington could backfire, generating strong nationalistic reactions in Mexico and stirring up traditional fears of U.S. intervention and dominance. Furthermore, from the perspective of U.S. security interests, it makes no sense to undermine the PRI when there is no obvious alternative to its rule.

The Congress and the U.S. media, however, do not necessarily share these views. Some lawmakers believe that U.S. and Mexican interests would be better served by supporting the right-of-center PAN. Given the economic crisis and the growing PAN challenge to PRI control in states that border on the United States, the media, while not necessarily for or against the PRI, have become more interested in covering Mexican elections. Their extensive reporting of electoral fraud in several state elections was viewed by many Mexicans either as interference in Mexican affairs, as part of a U.S. government conspiracy to pressure Mexico into changing its Central American policies that the U.S. Government finds objectionable, or both.

As long as Mexico is beset with economic difficulties, political discontent and demands for democratization will grow. So will the interest in Mexico on the part of U.S. citizens and the U.S. media. There is nothing that the U.S. Government can or should do to limit such interest. The world has changed and no country, including Mexico, can isolate itself easily from the rest of the world without taking steps that would be damaging in other ways.

Despite what the Mexican government may believe, increased scrutiny of the electoral process by the U.S. media is in Mexico's interests. It puts the PRI under pressure to eliminate corruption and fraud, to run better candidates and generally to be more attuned to the varied electorate that it claims to represent. Without such pressure, the PRI might have insufficent or no incentive to initiate reform. And while the party might be able to maintain its control for a period of time without changing, in the end its declining legitimacy and support would negatively affect its ability to govern.

Were that to occur, it is far from clear how events would play out. One possibility would be increased repression. Another would be the PRI's shift to a left-wing, populist, nationalistic, and anti-U.S. stance. The implementation of policies that would enhance the PRI's image as the party of social justice, combined with strong criticism of the United States, would restore some of the party's lost legitimacy, at least temporarily. Nevertheless, an extreme turn to the left or to the right probably could not be sustained indefinitely without provoking either civil war or a military takeover.

Fears of a military coup were rife during the last days of the Echeverría and López Portillo administrations, when it seemed as if both presidents had lost their psychological and political balance. The fears proved unfounded, in large part because everyone knew that Mexico would soon be governed by another president. If a weakened PRI were to be displaced by the Mexican military, however, it is not certain that order could be restored. A great deal would depend on the relative activism or passivity of the Mexican population.

The Mexican political system, however, remains far from collapse; it is in a period of transition. Whether it proves successful in restoring economic growth while maintaining political stability depends mainly on the behavior of its leaders, especially on their economic policies. If Mexico's leaders implement the necessary reforms too slowly, the economy will continue to deteriorate. If they move too fast, they could be destabilizing. The thorny problem confronting them is to define what constitutes change that is neither too slow nor too rapid.

U.S. policy should continue to focus on helping Mexico recover economically, for economic health is the key to success in other areas. A growing economy will reduce tensions and conflict in Mexico, as well as between Mexico and the United States. This, in turn, will facilitate the transition toward a more open and democratic political system—the goal of many Mexicans, including important government officials.

The Choices Facing Mexico

Jorge G. Castañeda

There is widespread support in Mexico for some kind of economic and political restructuring, but no consensus regarding exactly what must be done. There is no evidence that Mexico will be able to "grow out of its debt," which is the basic rationale for the economic austerity programs and efforts to liberalize the economy. Democratization is not a grass-roots demand. Nor does it necessarily mean the same thing to Mexicans as it does to Americans. To avoid a nationalistic backlash, the United States should refrain from exerting any kind of pressure on Mexico to liberalize its economy or its political system.

MEXICO IS CLEARLY NEARING a watershed in its history. It is increasingly evident to significant sectors of Mexican society that many of the ways and customs with which the country has lived comfortably and progressed remarkably over the past half-century are becoming more difficult to sustain. But if there is growing agreement on the need for change, and even on the broad direction change should take, there is no meaningful consensus as to the pace, the priorities, and the specifics of Mexico's needed *aggiornamento*. Perceptions and opinions differ as to what should be done about the four most important issues facing Mexico today: the debt crisis, the need for economic modernization, the country's democratization, and the role of the United States in each of these three matters. What follows is an overview of the terms of this debate, which will occupy centerstage in Mexican politics in the coming years.

The Debt Crisis

In the opinion of many Mexicans, the nearly $110 billion foreign debt is the overriding issue facing planners. Solving Mexico's debt crisis will not automatically solve its other problems, but at this stage it does seem clear that none of the other problems can be solved unless the debt crisis is solved first or, at least, solved at the same time as these other problems.

From a short-term economic standpoint, it makes little difference whether Mexico contracts new debt in order to pay the same amount of interest or whether it negotiates lower interest payments, allowing it to cut back on borrowing. The immediate net transfer of resources would be the same. From a political standpoint, however, there is a world of difference between these two options. Among Mexicans outside the government the prevailing view is that the first option (i.e., piling new debt onto old loans) is not a workable solution. Public opinion seems to have a point: It is difficult to understand how a debt problem can be solved by contracting more debt. The government is increasingly perceived as being incapable of dealing with the problem, as well as incapable of standing up to the international financial powers that be. Indeed, the government is viewed as simply accepting the terms dictated by these institutions and extracting as many concessions as possible within the framework of those terms. The second option, (i.e., negotiating a substantial reduction in interest payments—through below-market interest rates or a significant write-off) would give the government a political boost: Mexicans would view their government as having stood up to foreign creditors, as having changed the rules of the game, and as having obtained serious long-lasting debt relief.

In addition to the political and economic problems posed by the different solutions to the debt crisis, there is a technical problem. Namely, will Mexico be able to obtain, on a yearly basis and over a sustained period of time, sufficient resources from abroad to allow it both to grow and to pay interest? The key words here are "sufficient resources" and "grow"—everything depends on how these terms are defined. The Mexican economy grew by barely 0.5% in 1987. This meager growth came after a severe economic contraction of at least four percent in 1986. Moreover, it is doubtful whether growth will continue in 1988 and 1989. If growth is defined as barely catching up with what was lost in previous years because of economic recession, then clearly the Mexican economy can grow and pay simultaneously. But if growth means what it has traditionally meant in Mexico—six or seven percent annually over a period of five, ten, or fifteen years—then obviously the Mexican economy will not be able to grow and pay simultaneously.

For now, Mexico is still suffering the consequences of a net negative transfer of resources (the difference between new lending and total debt service outflows): it will have transferred some $2–3 billion abroad in 1986 and 1987, the two years covered by the recent agreement. To achieve high levels of growth for a sustained period of time, Mexico needs substantially more money than is being provided by recent restructuring, as well as significant *positive* transfers of resources. Given the extraordinary difficulties of achieving even the relatively low growth targets stipulated in current agreements and the enormous pressure that American financial authorities were obliged to exert on the private commercial banks, the IMF, and the World Bank to have them come up with just the amount of money necessary for 1986 and 1987, it is improbable that Mexico will obtain over the next five or ten years the necessary resource transfers to both grow and pay. The solution to the debt problem, then, clearly lies in a drastic reduction of interest payments, or of debt service in general.

That being the case, the government seems to have no alternative but to negotiate a write-off of between 30 and 50 percent of its debt to reflect the actual value of Mexican debt obligations on the secondary market. If this operation were spread over a ten-year period, the individual write-offs for each of the largest American banks would not be unmanageable, and the effect on the Mexican economy would be extremely favorable: both the ratio of debt to gross national product (GNP) and the ratio of debt service to export earnings would decline. The trick is to obtain such a solution without destroying Mexico's creditworthiness for the future.

There is no consensus on this issue in Mexico today. Government officials, among others, clearly put creditworthiness—the possibility of obtaining further credits in the future—above all other considerations. They attribute Mexico's problem to the very structure of its economy, rather than to the net transfer of resources abroad. In other words, if Mexico can restructure its economy, maintain its creditworthiness, and obtain funds from other sources, such as foreign investment, it can grow out of debt. The problem, of course, is that since 1982, Mexico has not grown out of debt; it has sunk more deeply into debt. There is no agreement as to whether this is because the economy has been restructured without effect, or because restructuring has not gone far enough or both. But there is no reason to believe that what could not be accomplished between 1982 and 1986 will be done in the near future.

Economic Modernization

The second issue on which Mexicans are divided is the country's need for economic modernization, an issue that stems directly from the debt crisis. By economic modernization, many people, including Mexican government officials, understand an opening-up of the economy to trade and to foreign investment, a reduction in state-provided subsidies, and a reduction in the size of the state-owned sector. But there are two sides to this question. Mexico's creditors—the monetary authorities of the industrialized countries, and international financial agencies—have said that if the Mexican economy were truly restructured and modernized, it could grow out of debt, achieve high levels of growth once again, obtain the necessary resource transfers to fuel those high levels of growth, and solve most of its medium-term problems. Many analysts in Mexico, on the other hand, believe that although measures to liberalize the economy must be undertaken, their effects, at least in the short term, are not as important as many people abroad consider them to be, and their political and economic shortcomings are significant.

This is undoubtedly the case with regard to the dismantling of Mexico's traditional international policy of protectionism. The Mexican economy has been highly protected for years, and this has entailed high levels of inefficiency, inflation, and technological backwardness. But opening up the economy while it remains stagnant, or with low reserves if it were to grow again, is not necessarily going to have a significant impact. Removing import licenses and replacing them with tariffs, or lowering tariffs, are not measures that in themselves signify that the Mexican economy will be more open if the demand for imports is not there, or if hard currency needed to import goods and services is not available.

The situation is similar with regard to foreign investment. The question is not whether Mexico is or is not open to foreign investment; the country has traditionally been a haven for foreign investment. The influx of foreign investment was heaviest shortly after the passage of the new foreign investment law in 1973. During 1979, 1980, and 1981, the years of the oil boom, well over $1.5 billion, and sometimes over $2 billion, entered the country each year. Foreign investment in Mexico depends less on the nature of relevant legislation than on whether or not the rest of the world has confidence in the country's political system and its economy. Changes in foreign investment laws may be seen as a sign of Mexico's willingness to go in a certain direction, and may eventually instill some confidence, but in themselves they are not going to make a substantial difference as far as actual investment plans are concerned. In the last analysis, Mexico may well have to reform its foreign investment legislation, if only because the issue has acquired symbolic value.

The question of eliminating or reducing state subsidies is also complex. Subsidies on consumer products are unending, bloated and, given the present scarcity of resources, unsustainable. But if such subsidies are slashed, industrial subsidies will also have to be cut. Since Mexican industry is already inefficient and inflationary, the reduction of industrial subsidies on energy, land, water, and other raw materials and intermediate goods would drastically increase their cost. The effect on the Mexican economy could be devastating. In some industries, cutting subsidies could force companies to become efficient, but in many others it would simply force companies out of business. It would be very dangerous to expose Mexican firms to foreign competition, by removing protectionist barriers, while simultaneously forcing them to face the problems arising from dramatic cuts in industrial subsidies, because the former measure forces them to be more competitive while the latter diminishes their competitiveness in the short run.

The same is true for direct consumer subsidies. There is no question that they must be slashed, but no Mexican government should do so unless it is willing to accept the consequences. If the government were to cut subsidies on transportation in Mexico City, for example, somebody else would have to pay: either the users themselves—particularly industrial workers who commute across town from their homes to their factories through a net reduction in their purchasing power—or the business community, through wage increases; or the government itself, which would end up paying for transportation in a different way. It is well and good to cut subsidies on public transportation in Mexico City if companies are willing to pay higher salaries or if labor is willing to accept a further reduction in real purchasing power. But after a 40 percent reduction in real wages over the past four years, it is difficult to imagine further wage reduction. The implication is that significant cuts in subsidies will inevitably result in real wage increases, exacerbating the already dangerous levels of inflation in Mexico over the coming months and years. This has already begun to a certain extent: in late 1986, there was an emergency increase of 21 percent. In 1987 wages were basically indexed to inflation, with hikes of up to 25% every 3 months. The challenge is to ensure that no new problems are created by implementing false solutions to old problems. Is it better to cut subsidies and increase real wages, or is it better to maintain subsidies as well as real wages at their existing levels? A case can be made for either of these two views, so it does not make a great deal of sense to believe that modernization measures—the reduction of consumer subsidies, in particular—have no downside and no negative consequences.

Reducing the size of the state-owned sector of the economy poses similar problems. To begin with, the problem is that most of the public sector is made up of the bureaucracy. Thus any real gains that might be achieved by closing down or by selling off inefficient state-owned companies, though perhaps not marginal, are not highly significant either. More importantly, once the selling off or closing down of state-owned firms begins, paradoxes immediately surface. The only firms that the private sector will buy are the money-making ones, but it does not make sense for the state to sell those firms because, by definition, it is not losing money on them in the first place. And nobody wants to buy the firms that the state *should* sell—the money-losing ones—for a very good reason: they lose money. This means that with few exceptions—such as expropriated bank-held firms and firms bailed out because of temporary problems—the only way to reduce the size of the state-owned industrial or service sector of the economy is to close down inefficient firms. Selling them off seems to be a somewhat utopian and remote possibility.

Other difficulties inherent in the sale of these properties are political, as well as economic. The economic aspect is more complicated than it would seem. In the short term, it probably costs more to shut down a company that is losing money than it does to keep subsidizing it. There are two reasons: first, the question of severance pay; and second, the debt carried by most state-owned companies. Workers in Mexico do not have unemployment insurance, but they are entitled to extraordinarily high severance pay. The labor code states that all employees laid off must be compensated with three months' salary plus twenty days' salary for each year of seniority. In state-owned companies, severance pay is disbursed by the government, and the amounts involved are enormous. In the long term, the state as a whole saves money by not having unemployment insurance. But in the short term, the costs of closing a company are far greater in many cases than the savings achieved by no longer subsidizing it. Furthermore, the debts owed by many state-owned companies have to be serviced even if the companies are closed down. Thus, the cash flow or deficit implications of closing down state-owned firms are not particularly favorable. In the long run, they are, but very few governments in the world, including the Mexican government, are in the business of dealing with the long term.

There is a second built-in deterrent to closing down state-owned firms which is political: It is doubtful that many employees laid off as a result of shutting down state-owned firms will find jobs in the short term. Once again, it can be argued that in the long run, the money saved will be invested elsewhere; that new, more productive, and better jobs will be created; and that more jobs will be available than there are now. But in the short run, the problem that the Mexican government—or any government for that matter—faces is what to do with the people who are laid off. In Western Europe, for example, where governments have set up social safety nets to cushion the hardships occasioned by industrial reconversion or reconstruction, the situation is very different. Mexico has no such social safety net, nor does it have the resources to establish one at present.

For all these reasons, and despite widespread support for economic modernization and restructuring, there is a great deal of debate and discussion going on in Mexico about each of these issues. Valid reasons exist for going ahead, as well as for not doing so. The same is true with regard to the country's democratization.

Democratization

The Mexican political system, which was created 50 years ago to govern a country that had been shaken by revolution and was essentially rural, agricultural, illiterate, backward, and scarcely populated, is no longer adequate for a nation of more than 80 million people who are essentially urban, working class or middle class, mostly literate, and linked to the rest of the world by modern telecommunications. Most Mexicans would agree that the problem is how to go about devising a new system that works and that will satisfy their yearning for further democratization.

There are a number of difficulties. Who is going to devise the new system? It is perhaps asking too much of a sitting government to develop a new system through which it will either lose power or be forced to share it. It is equally improbable that a ruling political system will devise a way to end its rule or to encourage competition and challenges to its rule. But the alternative—pressure from below—does not seem to exist in Mexico today. There is no widespread, active, and explicit clamor for the democratization of the country. Most Mexicans would prefer democratization, and a significant number of Mexicans reject the existing political system, but there is not a tremendous amount of pressure demanding the creation of a new political system. Some public demands for democratization have emerged in the northern states, but they tapered off quickly once it became apparent that the government would not give in. Something new is needed but nothing new is emerging, and the problems arising from this contradictory situation are more and more severe. These problems are reflected in paradoxical situations in many northern states and in some southern states (notably Oaxaca). On the one hand, both electoral competition and instances and perceptions of electoral fraud are increasing; on the other hand, the rates of abstention and non-participation in elections are also growing dramatically. People are voting in a different way, but they are also voting less and less. The implications of this for the democratization process are unclear.

The Role of the United States

The United States exerts an important influence on each of the three large issues facing Mexico today: the debt crisis, economic modernization, and the democratization of the political system. More importantly, it is perceived by most Mexicans as having a stake, an interest, and a role to play in solving these problems. On the debt crisis, for example, former Federal Reserve Board Chairman Paul Volcker and Treasury Secretary James Baker clearly played a key role in compelling Mexico, its creditors, and the international agencies to accept the present policy of lending Mexico more money to meet payments on its loans, but to lend the new money on better terms than those on which previous loans were made. To the extent that Mexicans today perceive the current level of debt servicing as unsustainable in the long term, because it effectively precludes higher levels of economic growth, they perceive the United States as playing a negative role in the debt crisis in the medium and long term, although it certainly has played a positive role in bailing out Mexico each time Mexico has encountered difficulties.

The question is whether those sectors in Mexico who think it best to side with the United States adopted the positions they hold on the debt issue because they believed that the United States would take those positions. The other question is whether those people who think that the correct stance on any Mexican issue is, by definition, one which is opposed to the American stance, really believe that the correct position on the debt issue is to oppose the constant rollover of Mexico's debt, and to take more radical steps such as declaring a moratorium on interest or debt payments. At any rate, what counts on the debt question is not so much what position the United States takes, though that is obviously relevant, but rather how that position fits into the debate on the debt issue within Mexico.

This is even more true with respect to the issues of economic modernization and democratization. In the case of economic modernization, there is a very clear perception in Mexico, especially within governing circles and the political establishment in general, that the United States is the strongest advocate of Mexico's so-called modernization. Some think that modernization is a good thing simply because the United States supports it; others think that it is a bad thing because the United States supports it, independently of the merits of modernization itself. Most importantly, the perception in Mexico that the United

States is pressuring the Mexican Government into carrying out these reforms—by making its loans to Mexico conditional on the implementation of these reforms, and by acting as the policeman, or watchdog, of this conditionality either directly or through the World Bank—is creating political tensions in Mexico. The reason is that even those Mexicans who favor economic modernization in one form or another are put into a very uncomfortable position: because they are perceived as supporting not economic modernization itself, but U.S. conditionality for Mexico. In this respect, overt and blatant American support for modernization and American pressure play a counterproductive role in Mexico today.

The same thing is true with regard to the democratization of Mexico's political system. Possibly as a result of former Ambassador John Gavin's support for, or in any case, his public appearance with members of, the National Action Party (PAN) in the north of the country during 1983 and 1984, the perception in Mexico is that the United States is actively pressuring for the creation of some sort of two-party system in Mexico.

This perception is having a negative effect in Mexico because many of those who strongly support democratization, whether it involves only elections or—as it should and as it will have to—a much wider process, are viewed as disguised supporters of a larger U.S. presence in Mexico. Many Mexicans actually believe that being in favor of honest elections and against fraud is tantamount to supporting greater U.S. involvement in Mexican politics. This is an extraordinarily difficult handicap for those in Mexico who support democratization. Once again, events in the United States have justified this perception: John Gavin's action, Jesse Helm's hearings, William Casey's obsession with Mexico and Oliver North's Mexican connection, among other things. The important point here is that as long as democratization is even remotely identified with American intervention in Mexican affairs— and to a large extent that is the case today—it is doubtful that a mass movement for greater democracy in Mexico will emerge. And until that movement surfaces, it is unlikely that any real pressure for democratization will develop.

In the final analysis, Mexico's problems do not lend themselves to simplistic, short-term solutions. Many on the left in Mexico argue that a moratorium is a simple and quick solution to Mexico's debt crisis, while many on the right contend that a few quick-fix remedies, including the modernization measures discussed above, will put the country back on the road to economic growth.

Some maintain that holding elections and accurately counting the votes will solve all of Mexico's problems, while the view in official circles is that "If we could just return to economic growth, everybody would stop bothering us about elections and electoral fraud and democracy." These viewpoints are oversimplified and false. There is no simple, quick remedy to Mexico's problems today.

There are reasons for being optimistic however. One of the most important reasons is the emergence of a "modernizing nationalism" movement in Mexico. It is still in an embryonic stage, with no broad support within the government, society, the political system, or the country. On each of the major issues, the proponents of modernizing nationalism take a different approach instead of reproducing traditional ideological alignments. On the debt issue, for example, they believe that the country should act unilaterally and decisively, regardless of a possible confrontation with the United States and Mexico's creditors. But in a break with the traditional left, they seem to feel that economic modernization is both desirable and inevitable, although they may disagree strongly among themselves on specific measures and the speed with which modernization should be carried out.

Lastly, and perhaps most importantly, proponents of "modernizing nationalism" believe that Mexico should go forward with democratization at the same time that it takes decisive action on its debt problem and on economic modernization. They also believe that democratization must be authentic and profound, extending beyond the electoral process to the press, the labor unions, the bureaucracy, the agricultural sector, and all realms of Mexican society. The "modernizing nationalism" faction maintains that these measures should be implemented simultaneously and, most importantly, without U.S. pressure or intervention. This is the somewhat unorthodox view that is emerging in certain Mexican circles today, one which could lead to a different vision for Mexico's future.

Part II
Politics in Transition

The Changing Role of the Private Sector

Luis Rubio F.

During the 1940s and 1950s, the Mexican government and private sector worked together to develop the country in accordance with a strategy known as import-substitution–industrialization. The government, through highly protectionist policies, shielded the private sector from international competition. The private sector, in turn, initially took advantage of its protected environment to establish and expand industrial and commercial enterprises. By the late 1960s, however, protection had become a way of life that hindered further economic growth. Instead of liberalizing the economy in the 1970s, President Luis Echeverría Alvarez borrowed abroad to sustain the old development model. His successor, President José López Portillo, used Mexico's oil wealth to do the same. Under President Miguel de la Madrid, who took office following the onset of the debt crisis and the fall in oil prices, Mexico was obliged to liberalize its economy. Despite resistance to these policies, Mexico must continue restructuring its economy in order to become globally competitive.

THE GROWING COMPLEXITY OF the Mexican and world economies makes it clear that the comfortable and mutually convenient relationship between the private sector and the government that existed in Mexico until the 1970s is a thing of the past. As Mexico's economy begins to participate actively in international markets, the role of the private sector will have to change drastically. Since Mexico's private sector is the creation of the government, this change will entail a radical transformation of the country's politics and culture. The challenge therefore is not merely to make the private sector competitive, but to make political decisions about the private sector's role in society.

The Government as Creator of the Private Sector

Mexico's history contrasts sharply with that of Europe. In Europe, the productive forces, faced with high levels of taxation, and regulatory and political conditions that impeded their development, gradually forced a radical transformation of the economic structure and of society

31

at large. The development of the productive forces brought about the development of capitalism.

Mexican capitalism—or the thwarted version that grew out of the Constitution of 1857—was not the result of the development of the productive forces. Mexico's historical evolution had not created an industrial bourgeoisie. The government, led by learned individuals who had stronger intellectual ties to the French, American, and Industrial revolutions than to Mexico's realities, was faced with a very simple—albeit dramatic—fact: there was no pressure for change from the productive forces.

Instead, during the second half of the nineteenth century, the Liberal Party took hold of the government and launched a political and economic program geared toward bringing about the development of capitalism. With the promulgation of the Constitution of 1857, and with the later adoption of specific measures and actions such as the expropriation of the church's properties, the government sought to modernize the country through industrial capitalism.

Thus, the Mexican government became the promoter, organizer, and virtual developer of the country's society and economy. The modernization of the country became the government's top priority, and with it came the development of the private sector. Private firms and groups had existed in Mexico before the second half of the nineteenth century, but it was not until the government assumed responsibility for developing the country that the conditions necessary for private-sector growth and development materialized.

The Government Becomes the Protector of the Private Sector

Since the private sector was, for all practical purposes, created by government policy, its development was to a large extent fashioned by the state. To promote the development of private enterprise, the government employed various devices, some of which were updated versions of the *encomienda* and *obraje,* the agricultural and industrial institutions created by the Spanish colonists through the concession of lands and native inhabitants to "investors." Concessions for the exploitation of lands and mines, and for the construction of roads, dams, bridges, and so forth, were the foremost instruments for the growth of private firms. Later on, the government resorted to tax incentives, protection from imports, direct subsidies, and subsidized credit to bolster the development of the private sector.

Until the 1930s, Mexico's private sector concentrated on commerce, agriculture, and mining. Even the Revolution of 1910 and subsequent upheavals did not significantly alter the pattern of private-sector activities. Mining and agricultural activities were, more often than not, globally competitive, and thus did not warrant or demand any unusual government protection or regulation.

Import-substitution–industrialization was first initiated as a result of the unavailability of imports during World War II, and later, through a well-conceived and comprehensive program, implemented during the late 1940s and early 1950s. It allowed hundreds of individuals to become *empresarios*, leading to rapid urbanization and growth of industrial employment. Import substitution entailed the manufacture of consumer products inside the country, generally with imported capital goods and within a protected environment. Protection from imports, together with direct and indirect subsidies, made it profitable for Mexicans to become industrialists. The first "captains of industry" were extremely conscious of their role and gained the respect of the authorities. As the private sector became more dependent on protectionist measures, however, the government began to dominate the relationship. Hence, the second- and third-generation *empresarios* were more subordinate to, and dependent on, the government, and more risk-averse. Foreign investors were significant participants in the process of import-substitution–industrialization, and they gradually adopted many of the attitudes that the private sector held about protection and risk.

Government investment in infrastructure, often through concessions to private firms, accomplished two key goals: (1) the establishment of clear-cut guidelines for investment in sectors and regions that the government had particular interest in fostering; and (2) the rapid attraction of private investment to those sectors and regions. These two goals not only provided an incentive for private investors, but also allowed the government to set national priorities and decentralize their implementation. The scheme was extremely effective, and it served to consolidate the government's role as organizer and orchestrator of society.

While industrialization was beginning to take place, the official political party, created in 1929 and given its current name, the PRI, in 1946, was becoming the country's main political institution. During the 1930s, the party incorporated most of the labor unions and peasant organizations, in an effort to strengthen the political system and to extend its political control over the country's main sectors and groups. The private sector, which the government considered strong and capable of organizing on its own, was incorporated by law into national chambers of commerce and industry—entities that would become instruments for the government's participation in, and control of, the private sector.

From the 1930s through the 1960s, the private sector was an effective agent of social change and economic growth. Closely following and complementing government investment in infrastructure, the private sector constituted a prime instrument for the achievement of the national goals set by each administration. In this way, Mexico became a largely industrial nation only a few years after it embarked on its industrialization program. While the partnership lasted, it enabled Mexico to sustain a growth rate of over 6 percent per year, on average, for over forty years. The government and the private sector were doing the jobs they were best qualified to do: investing in infrastructure and investing in production, respectively.

The Consequences of Protection

The protection and subsidization policies that characterized import-substitution–industrialization served their original purpose of creating and consolidating an industrial economy through the private sector. By the 1960s, Mexico had relatively strong industrial, banking, and trade sectors, with capable management teams and well-trained labor forces. The close working relationship between the private sector and the government—which operated in the context of a stable macroeconomic environment and very favorable external conditions—allowed Mexico to more than double the size of its economy every decade from the late 1940s on. In thirty years Mexico had built its private industry virtually from scratch. That accomplishment was not to last for long, however.

Forty-odd years of protection from imports introduced distortions into the economy. Over the years, the initial purpose of protection—to foster competitiveness—was forgotten, and protection became a way of life, as well as the conditioning factor of economic survival. Devices to secure protection for domestic firms, as well as power for the country's bureaucrats, proliferated.

A favorite mechanism was the creation of government offices, departments, and *subsecretarias*. These offices regulated competition, promoting market-sharing agreements among producers. Inevitably, these mechanisms eliminated incentives to increase productivity, to reinvest profits, and to become efficient and compititive—all at the expense of the consumer. These mechanisms also institutionalized the practice of solving the *empresarios*' problems through direct subsidies, import permits, concessions, or—the ultimate support scheme—the purchase or absorption of failing firms. Thus, the private investor, whether or not he was committed to building a globally competitive industry, became fully dependent on bureaucratic goodwill.

The excessively long period during which protection and subsidization prevailed hindered the development of new, globally competitive industrial sectors. This environment strengthened the government's participation in the economy—adding to its role as creator and protector of the economy the role of savior of failing industries—and fostered the colonial values of property, rather than those of productive competitiveness, as core beliefs of private-sector firms.

The Changing Role of Government in the Economy

By the late 1960s, the cozy relationship between the government and the private sector had created two fundamental structural problems. One was the fact that the domestic market was not large enough for the country's industry to attain sufficient economies of scale to manufacture products at world standards of price and quality. There was a compelling economic need to change course by gradually reducing protective mechanisms and exposing domestic industries to competition from imports.

Growth during the 1950s and 1960s had been possible because agricultural exports had provided foreign exchange to finance industrial imports. By the late 1960s, however, population growth and declining productivity had reduced Mexico's foreign-exchange earnings. Another impediment to future growth was the size of the market, which entailed high unit costs and low global competitiveness—at a time when countries such as Korea, Japan, and Brazil were launching export-driven patterns of growth. During the late 1960s and early 1970s, therefore, a major debate about liberalizing imports took place in Mexico, mostly within the government. Paradoxically, the economy's strength during this period was probably the greatest obstacle to liberalization; few parties perceived any urgency to liberalize.

The other structural problem was more political in nature. Allowing free competition would gradually reduce the government's ability to set guidelines for development. Once a firm has to measure itself vis-à-vis the world market, its prime considerations have to be profitability and long-term development—concepts that contrast radically with the history of Mexico's economy. Significant government participation in the economy gives rise to a politically active private sector, and vice versa. Because economic decisions were heavily politicized, private-sector firms became political lobbyists. Entrepreneurs found it paid to exert pressure on government officials, rather than to attain an outstanding economic performance; this naturally led private sector organizations to become political entities. Eventually this resulted in ever-growing political confrontation between private-sector organizations and the government.

Given the economic need to liberalize the economy and the reluctance of many government officials to do so for political reasons—as well as heavy pressure from private firms not to liberalize—the government had to change its policy. This conclusion was reinforced by the political upheavals of 1968, in which many groups manifested their displeasure with the uneven distribution of the benefits from economic growth. The government's refusal to liberalize and its simultaneous appeasement of the political tensions that surfaced in 1968 led to even greater government participation in the economy, as well as to a break in the government's traditional role as rector of economic activity.

The new approach was one of make-believe: to maintain economic growth (without liberalizing), while reducing political tensions. The government of Luis Echeverría Alvarez (1970–76) opted for increased government spending to attain the twin objectives of augmenting the size of the market while satisfying the needs of those groups that believed they had not benefited from economic growth. Increased government spending, financed by inflation and foreign indebtedness, would eventually lead to the disaster of 1982, but for several years it was the foremost instrument of government policy.

The government and the private sector were united in at least one major—albeit disastrous—goal: to attempt to perpetuate the cozy environment that had characterized the country's economy in previous decades. Although the private sector, particularly industry, did not necessarily agree with the means used to attain that goal (i.e., an increased government role in the economy), it cannot shirk responsibility for having supported that objective to the very last.

To sustain industrial growth, the government began in 1970 to stimulate the domestic market through rapidly growing deficit-spending. Public spending increased, from about 20 percent of gross domestic product (GDP) during the 1960s to around 34 percent in the late 1970s. From 1972 through 1981, artificial stimulation of consumption and massive inflows of foreign exchange (the result of foreign indebtedness and oil exports) fueled economic growth. By the early 1980s, however, Mexico found itself faced with a deep recession, extremely high levels of foreign debt and, above all, an industrial program that did not—and cannot—work in the 1980s.

Together with a significant increase in spending, the government incorporated into its role four key political features: (1) as inflation soared, price controls gradually led to virtual expropriations of many private firms—in addition to specific expropriatory decisions; (2) government rhetoric directed against the private sector transformed the once close relationship between the private sector and the government; (3) the shift from government investment in infrastructure to investment in parastatal firms often pitted the government against private firms and impeded future growth by failing to develop the country's infrastructure; and (4) increased government spending to appease political tensions not only made the economy more complex and government decisions about it more discretionary, but also forced the government to undertake all sorts of maneuvers to maintain political control and economic growth. All these features set the stage for growing confrontation with the private sector and, eventually, a financial crisis.

By the latter half of the 1970s, the government's presence in the economy had become ubiquitous. Not only did the government increase in size, but its attributes grew dramatically. Through the use of permits, concessions, regulations, and controls, and through sheer size, the government wielded enormous economic clout. Ironically, the instrument that had served the government's goals so well—investment in infrastructure—took a back seat to investment in industrial enterprises. Some of the latter were new ventures, while many others were the result of takeovers of failed private firms. Meanwhile, the growth of parastatal firms put additional pressure on the financial markets for funds—formerly available mostly to the private sector. The perceived need to protect the domestic market and industrial firms and to maintain political dominance led to ever-increasing regulations, price controls, subsidies to producers and consumers, and the like. Protection went so far as to unite the government and the private sector against foreign investment (in order to avoid new competition). Moreover, it allowed the government to justify its practice of allowing select foreign firms into the country while refusing entry to their competitors.

Although some degree of political tension between the public and the private sector is normal in any society, the tension in Mexico in the 1970s erupted into direct confrontation. The change in the role of the government and, above all, the increasing politicization of the economy, drove the private sector to organize itself politically. In 1975, for example, the private sector created the Consejo Coordinador Empresarial (Business Coordinating Council), a political entity aimed at coordinating the private sector's policies.

The growing polarization between the private sector and the government in the 1970s culminated in the expropriation of Mexico's private banks in 1982. Since then, the private sector has split on the question of the government's (and, for that matter, the private sector's) future role. Some, particularly small *empresarios*, claim that nothing short of a radical break with the past (i.e., an end to "interventionist" government) will work; many of them have joined or supported the opposition National Action Party (PAN). Others claim that the expropriation of the banks was an isolated event, and that the country should go back to business as usual.

When the de la Madrid administration took over in 1982, it realized that the relationship between the government and the private sector had to be redefined. In the same month that it took office, the administration introduced an amendment to the Constitution clarifying the respective roles of the government and the private sector. The amendment legitimizes the private sector, gives primacy to the government over the economy, and introduces the concept of "rectorship of the state." Although the amendment simply formalized what had been a reality for many years, the private sector interpreted the amendment to mean that it was being displaced by the government. Apparently, the private sector believed that ratifying what was already a reality was not only the exact opposite of what was required, but also contradicted its own perceived role. Interestingly, few, if any, private-sector leaders had realized that the role of the government in the economy had grown as a direct result of the private sector's reluctance to liberalize in the 1960s.

The current administration has attempted to reduce the size of the parastatal sector and cut public spending, to liberalize imports, and to put the economy back on the growth track through "structural changes" (e.g., correcting imbalances, eliminating some of the hindrances to production, liberalizing domestic prices and doing away with burdensome regulations). It decided to launch a new full-scale development policy to replace the exhausted import-substitution–industrialization approach, but its specific nature and shape remain to be worked out. Thus, despite the commitment to change, much more remains to be done.

Moreover, the administration has faced major opposition within its own ranks, as well as opposition from labor and the private sector. The latter, however, is divided on liberalization: many firms now realize that liberalization is unavoidable and are concentrating on slowing the pace of liberalization. Not all industrial sectors, however, are equally protected or subsidized, given differences in (a) their objective need for protection; (b) their clout; and, more importantly, (c) the degree of political sensitivity of their particular product. Consequently, there are significant differences among the *empresarios*. Many textile firms, for instance, are very competitive—and face problems similar to those of their foreign counterparts. Most manufacturing firms, however, have enjoyed a protected market where agreements and understandings among competitors—usually brokered by the government—took away the incentive to compete on the basis of efficiency and quality. Hence, many *empresarios* have been more successful because of conditioning factors in the environment, rather than because of their skill or savvy.

The Complexity and Heterogeneity of the Private Sector

In many instances, direct government actions, such as concessions or contracts, led to the creation of industrial concerns; in others, however, general macroeconomic conditions fostered the establishment and development of private firms. Those concerns that predated the first government efforts to develop a private sector—many of the large Monterrey industrial firms, for instance, or the Banco Nacional de México and the Banco de Londres y México (Sérfin)—prospered as a result of government policy, but were not created by it.

Over the years, three types of private concerns emerged, each with its own distinctive relationship to the government: (1) large groups that depend heavily on the government for contracts, influence, and investment; (2) large groups relatively independent of the government; and (3) thousands of small and medium-size firms that have neither influence nor a strong relationship with the government. Of course, the three categories overlap, and some firms have changed from one category to another (e.g., some of the Monterrey firms that had previously boasted of their independence became extremely dependent on the government in the late 1970s, essentially because of their dependence on prices set by the government—e.g., oil, steel, etc.). Nonetheless these categories help to explain the nature and the extent of the change that is required in Mexico's economy. Firms in the first group must undergo a radical shift in their traditional mentality; they must learn to think in terms of a global economy rather than a small and protected national economy. Firms in the second group only require a change in focus, for they have always been aware of the need to think in global terms. Small and medium-sized firms, in spite of their declarations to the contrary, are actually much better at adapting to and surviving in a competitive environment. To survive in Mexico's traditionally oligopolistic economy, they have had to be flexible.

These broadly defined clusters of private-sector companies and leaders take very different attitudes toward liberalization. Groups dependent, directly or indirectly, on government contracts or goodwill usually oppose reductions in government spending and the liberalization of the economy. They claim that liberalization goes against the national interest. Groups relatively independent of government regulations or contracts are usually more in favor of the liberalization. Although both groups include big as well as small firms, the smaller firms in each group have tended to produce the most militant private sector leaders: those radically opposed to the government policy, as well as those extremely dependent on the government's protection and who are, therefore, staunch supporters of any policy.

These differences illustrate that the private sector is not monolithic, that it does not act in a concerted fashion, and that relationships with the government vary from firm to firm. The relationship of individual firms and private-sector organizations to the government is therefore extremely complex. This complexity, if nothing else, would be sufficient to warrant a different economic policy, for it shows that there is much latitude not only in terms of liberalization and providing temporary protection for failing firms, but also in terms of the private sector's potential role in Mexico's economic development. These are ultimately political decisions.

Can Mexico's Industry Become Competitive?

The conditions that enabled the Mexican economy to function effectively from the 1930s onward have ceased to exist. Not only has the world economy changed dramatically, but the structure of Mexico's industry has changed as well. The kind of industry that sustained economic growth for over forty years is not the type of industry that can insure future economic growth. Like any other economy, Mexico's economy must specialize in those industrial sectors where it can attain levels of efficiency and quality that compare favorably with those of the other nations in the world market.

Because the industrial policy of past decades is hindering Mexico from attaining its previously high growth rates, it must be abandoned. The de la Madrid administration has designed a program of "structural change" and "industrial reconversion" aimed at making Mexico's industry world-competitive. That program, however, fails to address the central problem, which is twofold: on the one hand, Mexico's economy requires increased competition to become competitive on international levels; on the other hand, competitiveness can be attained only by competing.

Under the current program, however, the bureaucracy will decide how, when, and how fast firms (mainly, but not exclusively, parastatal firms) can or will be "reconverted." In theory, "reconversion" makes the company ready for competition, but in practice a "reconverted" entity is not always world-competitive. There is no detailed program for reconversion of private-sector firms. Private firms are expected to adjust to competition through gradual liberalization.

International examples abound to prove that the only way a firm can become competitive is by competing. The role of the government should be to create the macroeconomic conditions necessary for that competition to take place. At the same time, however, the government should make public a definitive schedule of effective liberalization so that companies are fully aware of the long-term implications of failure to adjust. The current government policy is aimed in the right direction, but it has been inconsistent and has not gone far enough. Moreover, the government has merely made adjustments to an old industrial policy, rather than formulating a new one.

The private sector must undergo a monumental transformation. Private industry has to adjust to a world environment where cozy agreements among competitors do not work, where a government can do little to save a firm, and where profitability is based on high volume and low margins, rather than the reverse. Above all, to compete internationally or, at least, to produce on a scale at which it will be competitive in the world market, the private sector will have to specialize in a few select industrial sectors rather than operate in all sectors of a protected economy. To be able to compete successfully once the economy has been liberalized, the private sector will require huge amounts of capital. Hence, liberalization might prove to be a far more effective inducement to the repatriation of capital than any number of useless controls and regulations.

In the public sector, the problem is, first, to develop a new philosophy, one that replaces that which has guided the government's actions for half a century, and second, to treat parastatal companies like other firms. To force firms to adjust to increased competition, Mexico must do away with its bloated bureaucracy which, for decades, has been trusted with controlling and regulating industrial growth. The philosophy of control will have to be replaced by one of free markets and macroeconomic, rather than sectoral, promotion.

For years, the government has shielded inefficient parastatal firms from competition by proclaiming them strategic or by giving them "priority" status. Making a firm efficient and productive is not equivalent to privatizing it. There are legitimate historical and political reasons for government ownership of certain key industries. But there is no justification for inefficiency in any sector of the economy—least of all in those sectors that are clearly capable of earning profits in the global market, such as oil, electricity, and communications.

Mexicans must make a fundamental political decision about the kind of society and economy they want a decade or two from now. Whether the private sector has a role in Mexico's future depends solely upon that key decision. If Mexicans should decide that the only useful role that the private sector could play in the 1990s is that of industrial entrepreneurship, then they must consciously and deliberately liberalize the market and radically change their industrial policy so as to reduce the regulatory role of the government.

The private sector may be an effective agent of one kind of development, and at the same time be completely useless in others. Therefore, to create conditions for one kind of development and then expect the private sector to perform in a way that does not correspond to those objective conditions is unrealistic. Increased productivity, improved quality, and new investment, cannot be achieved in a protected economy; they can only occur in a liberalized economy. Like any other sector in society, the private sector must operate in conditions, environmental and otherwise, created by the government. Hence, the government's principal challenge is to define the future shape of Mexican society; everything else would follow.

The government could redefine its relationship with the private sector such that it would set general guidelines and, through investment in infrastructure, set clear priorities. Such a decision would imply the virtual elimination of existing government regulations and controls, which do not allow for sustained economic growth, and the substitution of indirect mechanisms of economic promotion.

Politically, economic growth is the only viable option. The choice is quite stark: either the economy modernizes or it will not grow. The challenge is daunting, but history has proved over and over that Mexico's political system is capable of undertaking major challenges. Hence, in spite of the enormity of the task ahead, the odds are quite favorable.

The Impact of Economic Crisis on the Mexican Political System

Soledad Loaeza

The economic crisis has had an important impact on electoral politics and on relations between the state and pressure groups. It has favored the right-of-center National Action Party (PAN), which represents mainly middle- and upper-class interests that have led the protest against the policies of the dominant Institutional Revolutionary Party (PRI). Although the PAN is good at electoral politics, it still has a bad grasp of the issues facing Mexico. This will keep it from constituting a viable alternative to the PRI. The economic crisis has also produced greater activity by pressure groups. This does not endanger Mexico's political stability, since protests against the government's performance have been channeled within established institutions. PRI's 1988 presidential candidate wants to continue the policies of the current administration, but it is not clear that he will have enough popular support to do so.

T HE CURRENT ECONOMIC CRISIS in Mexico has had an unquestionable impact on the country's political life and institutions. Not only has it submitted the system to the strains of constant negotiations between the government and business organizations, trade unions, opposition parties, and even the Catholic Church, but economic deterioration also has injected what seems to be a very acute new political awareness into large sectors of Mexican society.

The open expression of criticism and disagreements has created a somewhat uncertain political situation, which is fluid, complex and contradictory. Discontent has been manifested mainly in capital flight and in electoral support for opposition parties, both to the right and to the left of the official party, the Institutional Revolutionary Party (PRI). However, the political system has not suffered a discontinuity comparable to the abrupt downturns in the economy since 1982.

Thus far, the political effects of the economic crisis seem to be related more to the rollback of the Mexican interventionist state than to a general rejection of the system. This limitation of the role of the state in society is a specific policy promulgated as a response to an ailing economy. Its effects have been felt in two key areas: in adjustments in the relations between the state and various pressure groups, and in the local electoral processes that have taken place in different states since 1983.

The ailing economy has stirred the traditionally weak opposition parties, especially the National Action Party (PAN). Economic troubles have helped the PAN increase the breadth of its political support, and this long-standing loyal opposition party has thus been projected to the forefront of political debate.

Present circumstances favor the PAN, rather than other opposition parties, principally because until now, the main protests against the system have come from the upper and middle classes. It is precisely from segments of these classes that PAN voters have been drawn. In some cases, however, such as in Chihuahua (where the PAN's gubernatorial candidate received strong support in the 1986 election), the PAN has also been backed by the urban lower class.

Given its historical origins, issues, and allies, the PAN represents the 20th-century conservative opposition within the Mexican context. The party had its origins in 1939 in the urban middle-class reaction against the populist policies of President Lázaro Cárdenas (1934–1940). Its purpose was to represent the interests of the private sector. Nevertheless, this objective was not fully realized, because in the mid-1940s, the Mexican state and an incipient private sector began a functional collaboration that would last for more than four decades. This situation put the PAN in the hands of militant Catholics who rejected anticlerical legislation and undertook the defense of the Church.

In 1939, as now, the main target of the PAN's criticisms was the official party, the PRI. The issues the PAN raised then were more or less the same as those it is raising today: the defense of the individual against the state, of private property, and of municipal autonomy, and the rejection of corruption and government control over political participation. These issues were not appealing to public opinion during the years when the dominant party and the Mexican version of a mixed economy guaranteed expansion and social mobility. However, they have been resurrected as a result of the discrediting of populism because of its association with the government of Luis Echeverría Alvarez (1970–1976), and, most of all, because of Jóse López Portillo's populist justification for the expropriation of the commercial banks. That decision and the circumstances under which it was taken help explain the popularity the PAN has enjoyed among private-sector groups.

The party is also favored because of its history of regular participation in elections, which has given it a solid reputation as a genuine and autonomous opposition party; by contrast, other parties, such as the Popular Socialist Party (PPS) and the Authentic Party of the Mexican Revolution (PARM), are viewed as mere instruments of the state. Thus, for the first time in more than 40 years of modest performance, in 1983, the PAN was thrust into the center stage of Mexican political debate as a serious challenger of the PRI. Municipal and state elections in Sonora, Nuevo León, San Luis Potosí, Durango, Chihuahua, Baja California, Sinaloa, and Puebla were occasions for the party to prove its new potential for mobilization. While this potential was not reflected in actual electoral victories, the impact on the political atmosphere was important. The PAN's strong showing exposed one of the central weaknesses of the Mexican political system: corrupt elections. Numerous incidents of electoral fraud on the part of PRI supporters were well-documented and publicized.

Contrary to custom, these elections were not surrounded by indifference. Their importance was magnified by the active support the PAN received from powerful local business and religious organizations. These groups participated in what some called a crusade for democracy against the central government and its policies of imposing decisions and candidates from above, without any consideration for local conditions and interests. In this sense, electoral opposition constituted a revolt within the states against the authoritarianism of Mexico City.

The states where the PAN mobilized wide electoral support share a number of characteristics: similar levels of economic development and standards of living, and large proportions of middle-class groups, which have played a decisive role in the electoral protest.

It is said that the middle classes have suffered most from the economic crisis, because of their vulnerability to inflation. However, this view minimizes the devastating effects the recession has had on the lower classes, particularly in terms of unemployment. Still, the middle-class protest seems to have originated in response to the dismal economic future the country faces and to the middle-class perception that privileges and advantages they obtained during the economic boom will be lost. The oil boom was especially beneficial to the middle classes, which until then had not known such prosperity. Statistics show that to the extent that there was any income redistribution during the years 1976–1982, it favored these middle sectors. Certainly, the

Echeverría and López Portillo governments gave first priority to the demands of these social groups, probably as a reaction to the severe political crisis that followed the repression of the university student movement in 1968. Between 1970 and 1982, the political and economic participation of the middle classes expanded dramatically, as evidenced by the development of a more critical press and electoral legislation aimed at promoting the participation of opposition parties, and by a general liberalization of political life.

The PAN's gains in local elections since 1983 seem to be, more than anything else, a sign of disapproval of government policies and of the PRI's reluctance to relinquish its virtual electoral monopoly. However, the party's growth in popularity does not imply that it is replacing the PRI, though it has served as a vote catcher to put pressure on the PRI. It is puzzling that purportedly modern opposition groups, to express their discontent, support a party that has changed less than the rest of Mexican society in forty years.

Perhaps to many voters, the PAN represents a means to democratize the political system, since in becoming a serious competitor of the PRI, it could prompt policy changes that reflect greater responsiveness to social demands—an indispensable characteristic of real democracy. Others consider the PAN a desirable alternative to the PRI because they see it as a plausible initiator of a conservative anti-statist revolution, which would make Mexico part of a more general global trend.

Despite the PAN's emerging visibility, this party has serious weaknesses. First of all, it has concentrated its attention on elections, ignoring the necessity of designing a convincing and realistic political and economic program. The *panistas* are shrewd in electoral matters, but when asked about other crucial subjects—such as unemployment, the external debt, or the international oil market—they give answers that are simplistic and reveal a poor grasp of the issues.

Second, the PAN's future seems to depend less on its capacity to appeal to a large number of voters than on its ability to maintain the support of powerful allies. The problem is, however, that these allies— business organizations and the Catholic hierarchy—can sidestep the PAN and appeal directly to the government to reach agreement on matters of more importance to them than which party wins the elections. This occurred during the election in the state of Sonora in 1985, when the PRI candidate negotiated with the local business community and obtained the support it had originally given to the PAN. Moreover, in February 1987, a group of more than 130 industrialists in Nuevo León created the Frente de Solidaridad Empresarial (Business Solidarity

Front) as a means of promoting their political participation independent of the PAN.

The Catholic Church does not seem ready to engage itself permanently with the PAN either, even though the party has made the Church's demands its own. In the last 15 years, the Catholic Church has made remarkable progress in the political arena. Its participation in public affairs is more frequent than ever and is widely publicized by the media. In this manner, the Church has sought to play an important role as an opinion leader in matters that are not directly related to religious concerns. Nevertheless, it has avoided identifying itself with any one particular political party, because doing so would belie its pretentions to represent the majority of Mexicans. By being tied up with a particular party, the Church would limit its own political freedom and lose its appeal to groups that do not identify with that party. It is crucial for the Church to keep the flexibility needed to maintain support in a diverse society. That is why, while the bishops in the north support the PAN, those to the south have adopted positions closer to leftist parties, and many others support the PRI. The clergy thus show a capacity to be flexible and also demonstrate a widespread willingness to actively participate in politics. Regardless of how the Church in Mexico aligns itself, its participation could prove disturbing, given the already fragile political situation. However, the Catholic Church is not ready to confront the state because, among other reasons, its relations with the government are friendly, and their dialogue remains uninterrupted.

Today, many contest the PRI's continued presence in power (it has been in power since 1929), but few consider it an illegitimate organization. The party's political predominance has been so entangled with Mexican modernization, the PRI must be considered not only a central element in Mexico's political culture, but both a central and controversial player in any discussion about democracy in the country. If the official party were a totalitarian organization, such discussion would be inconceivable.

In spite of appearances, however, the PRI's role in Mexican politics is limited, because it is mainly an electoral machine and seldom intervenes in the day-to-day decision-making process. The PRI is currently in trouble because government policies contradict its populist traditions—the only justification it had for controlling some of the more important worker and peasant organizations. The official party has supported the government's economic policies and has remained loyal, but it is only natural for the PRI to react strongly against losing elections.

The PRI's response to the PAN's northern offensive reveals a degree of insecurity not entirely justified. In spite of the image projected by the media, the *panista* opposition still has to demonstrate that it represents a national force; in the last presidential elections, in 1982, the PAN obtained less than 17 percent of the total turnout. In fact, the real problem for the PRI is not so much the strength of the opposition, but its own lack of credibility. In this sense, the PAN has employed shrewd tactics since 1983, including denouncing electoral fraud before it actually occurred, so that in every state campaign, its strength lay in the PRI's bad reputation rather than in its own independent appeal.

The traditional dominance of the PRI poses another problem in terms of an effective opposition in Mexico. For many years, the party has been the recruiting ground for the political elite and for public administrators, and viable alternatives for the provision of political leadership have not yet surfaced. This points to one of the major difficulties the opposition parties face: They have simply been unable to produce an attractive and convincing leadership at the national level. Given these circumstances, many Mexicans believe that the consequences of change, even brought about by elections, are unpredictable and undesirable.

Because of the difficulties faced in implementing reform from without, some PRI members have attempted it from within. In the last year, currents of opinion have appeared within the party demanding a democratization—that is, an open process for the selection of the party's candidates. From these the most serious challenge came from a group led by Cuauhtemoc Cárdenas, son of the legendary president, Lazaro Cárdenas, called the Corriente Democrática. This rallied some well-known members of the PRI's left wing, such as former minister of Education and President of the PRI itself, Porfirio Múñoz Ledo. The Corriente Democrática intended to remain within the party, and at the same time criticize harshly its methods of internal selection of candidates, as well as the present government's economic policy, mainly the foreign debt policy.

The PRI reacted very strongly against the Corriente, and on various occasions condemned the "divisionism" and "act of indiscipline" it represented. Nevertheless, the group remained active as a PRI faction until the name of the PRI's new candidate for the presidency was announced in early October 1987. Then Cárdenas decided to campaign as an independent candidate, with the support of the Authentic Party of the Mexican Revolution (PARM).

One might expect that the consequences of the economic crisis—a sharp drop in living standards, rising unemployment, and worsening social inequalities—would strengthen leftist parties, given their commitment to defending the lower classes. Surprisingly, however, the Left has not gained meaningful support. This failure demonstrates the effectiveness of the PRI relative to its rivals on the Left. Unlike the PAN, the former Unified Socialist Mexican Party (PSUM) (which has now merged with the Mexican Workers Party (PMT) to form the Mexican Socialist Party (PMS), the Socialist Workers Party (PST), and the Revolutionary Workers Party (PRT) have not been successful in capitalizing on resentment and discontent, although some of them have won elections in southern states. Their influence has expanded nevertheless, if only through their presence in the Chamber of Deputies, which has become an important forum for the expression of domestic criticism and dissent.

Thus, economic crisis has created a fluid and relatively uncertain political situation, which has been characterized by the emergence of growing political pluralism: Business and religious organizations, unions, intellectuals, and middle-class associations now have a greater tendency to express their opinions in areas that affect their interests. This increased participation has not undermined Mexico's political stability because the PRI has adapted to the expanded participation and has not tried to suppress protest and the dissenting views.

In the last 20 years, the Mexican state has followed a reformist course aimed at gradually recognizing political pluralism and promoting more effective competition for power. The main characteristic of these reforms has been greater tolerance of independent political participation. Thus, several organizations, including unions and political parties (to mention the most obvious), have been integrated into the system. This enlargement of the political arena since the early 1970s has prevented the development of new sources of instability, at the same time that it has assured orderly change. Paradoxically, these reforms have focused on elections, yet it is in the electoral process that the government's main political weakness lies.

As a consequence, though the economic crisis has not given rise to new demands for political participation, it has given independent groups a sense of urgency. The issue has not been the necessity for change—regarding which all those involved in or concerned with Mexican politics seem to agree—but the pace at which such change should be implemented and the direction it should take. This issue presents one of the more serious dilemmas the present government has to face: On the one hand, political stability is a necessary ingredient of any stabilization program, but on the other hand, economic hard times make political reform more difficult, particularly in a situation of international vulnerability.

Important as political discontent is, until now, protest against the government's performance has been channeled within established institutions. These have not been overwhelmed by protest, and the process itself has had an important stabilizing effect on the fluid political situation I have described.

Adding to the Mexican political system's domestic difficulties is what might be called the "American factor." Mexico has become a subject of increased interest in the United States, as one of the main suppliers of illegal drugs Americans consume, as a supplier of unwanted migrants and cheap labor, and—in the view of the more hawkish sectors in the United States—as the ultimate target of Soviet strategy in Latin America. While a discussion of these perceptions is beyond the scope of this paper, it is worth pointing out that the Mexican economic crisis made many groups of American public opinion suddenly aware of the existence of their southern neighbor and of its problems. Some of these problems seem so unmanageable, that there is a widespread feeling that Mexico's future cannot be taken for granted anymore, and that Mexico is increasingly becoming a liability to the United States. Concerns about the stability of the political system have been discussed both in the U.S. Congress and in the mass media, and there were severe criticisms of prominent Mexican public officials and of Mexican political institutions and practices.

Regardless of the ideological, political, or economic motivations of these denunciations, their impact on the Mexican political situation has been considerable, disturbing, and perhaps unforeseen. These attacks not only are further proof of Mexico's international vulnerability, but they also have helped undermine Mexican confidence in the ability of domestic political institutions to effect an economic recovery. To the extent that American interests play a role in this recovery, the doubts expressed in the United States about Mexico's future may delay economic recovery. But the important problem lies in the consequences of external undermining of a political system at a time when such criticism reinforces domestic pressures. This could be devastating for the development of a viable and locally acceptable political alternative.

The American factor is not a policy toward Mexico, but the compounded effect of apocalyptic reports in the American press and the statements made in the U.S. Congress or by government officials in Washington. This inevitably becomes an element in domestic politics given Mexico's dependency on the United States. Since 1983, in spite of many contradictions, American criticisms converged in a strongly negative judgment of Mexican authorities and institutions. They put the system under fire, baring the darker side of Mexican politics and adding to the feeling of discomfort and unease that financial and natural disasters have provoked in wide sectors of the population. The American factor magnified the deficiencies and weaknesses of the system in the eyes of Mexicans themselves.

By distorting the sense of political protest and exaggerating the strength of the electoral opposition, American opinion makers have tended to predict political disruption in Mexico. For example, during the 1986 state elections in Chihuahua, the American press at times gave the impression that a state of political emergency existed, a perception not shared by most Mexicans. This attitude pressured the government, and many Mexicans perceived it as a policy formulated in Washington to provoke political change in Mexico.

The American factor could, in fact, jeopardize the chances for political reform in Mexico, because when changes are perceived to be the result of foreign interference in domestic affairs, they kindle nationalistic passions and may produce pressures to maintain the system intact as a demonstration of self-determination. Sovereignty could become an excuse to reject change. Thus, the American factor could, paradoxically, reduce the chances for success of those in Mexico who are pressing for more democracy.

The damaging effects of the American factor could limit and influence political choices, and also add new rigidities to the system. The American factor explicitly contains criticisms, but also implies a well-defined set of solutions: a liberal economy, a two-party system, and weak interest groups. These solutions seem to encompass a determination of the timing, scope, and direction of political change, in a manner that would follow in the footsteps of the national experiences of the United States and, more recently, the Philippines. History, however, teaches that if political change is to last, it must come as a response to domestic developments, and not external pressure.

The Functioning of the Mexican Political System

In the first months of 1987, the Mexican political system was facing mounting pressure from powerful unions, whose ability to contain their members' demands depends on their credibility as representatives of the workers' interests. To be functional to the system, unions first have to be functional to their members. Until now, these unions have supported the economic policies of the government; but inflation is eroding family budgets and the workers' patience as well. If 1986 was a year of electoral mobilization for the Mexican political system, 1987 began with a labor mobilization; as a result, 1988 may bring unprecedented competition for the presidential elections. In this case, economic policies may need to be revised.

As the presidential succession approached, it could have been thought that this context of changing political balance and contradictory pressures would force a modification of the traditional mechanism for the selection of the official party's candidate for the presidency of the republic. Nevertheless, and in spite of some formal changes, the candidacy of Carlos Salinas de Gortari, former Minister of Planning and Budget, launched by the PRI in the first days of October, obeyed the long-standing rules of a decision taken from above.

Although Salinas de Gortari has started his campaign trying to inaugurate a new style in politics, more open and direct, for which his youth is an advantage, his main strength is still de la Madrid's support. Probably one of the fundamental reasons why Salinas was chosen was that he represents continuity, not so much of personal power, but of a long-term project of political and economic transformation of Mexico, which has been designed by the group who came to power in 1982. As Planning and Budget Minister, Salinas was a key figure in the implementation of the economic policies of the last five years, and as such he became a favorite target for union discontent and protest. As a matter of fact, their open opposition to his candidacy, expressed in various ways during 1987, was no deterrent to his becoming the PRI's candidate.

However, Salinas de Gortari's candidacy represents the determination of a group within the political elite to carry out profound changes, relating mainly to the scope of the State's authority, intended to lead the country toward its own ideal of what a modern Mexico should be. Nevertheless, this project may encounter, and has already encountered, substantial opposition from vested interests represented by powerful national unions or the PRI itself. Also, this modernization project has yet to find a wide basis of consensus within Mexican society. This goal may prove unattainable in a situation in which medium-term economic and social perspectives are less than optimistic.

Questions and Cautions About Mexico's Future

David Ronfeldt

Fears about imminent political instability in Mexico are probably unwarranted. The conventional indicators of political breakdown are less relevant to Mexico, a country of "compatible contradictions" characterized by a unique political culture, a strong and cohesive nationalism, and a perceived absence of better alternatives. Furthermore, the current crisis was precipitated by external shocks; it could thus be resolved by developments outside of Mexico. A big challenge, however, remains the fragmentation of the elite and the need to reestablish balance among its various factions. The military also appears to be increasing its influence, but it is probably only modernizing its relationship to the PRI. These and other changes could complicate relations with the United States. But bilateral tensions could be managed if each nation committed itself to act responsibly toward the other.

THESE ARE OMINOUS TIMES for Mexico and U.S.–Mexican relations. During 1986, bashing, doomsaying, and threat-mongering about Mexico at times reached feverish proportions in the U.S. media. Such alarmist thinking has not permeated the mainstream of professional policy-oriented analysis in academe and elsewhere. Yet many U.S. experts who for years have been deliberately sympathetic toward Mexico have turned unusually pessimistic about Mexico's future, and, partly with good reason, have voiced critiques and tough U.S. policy views that one would not have heard from them a few years ago.

Three political uncertainties in particular have plagued the analytical and policy debates about what is happening in Mexico:

- Is Mexico as a whole headed for serious instability?
- Is Mexico's political system still viable?
- Is the Mexican military gaining influence?

In many ways Mexico is a mysterious, impenetrable, and even unknowable country—to its own people as well as to outside observers.

53

When things seem to be going well, these characteristics may serve to enhance expert optimism about Mexico's future. But when things seem to be going badly, these same characteristics make it much easier for experts to turn pessimistic. No wonder so much uncertainty and controversy surrounds these questions.

Rather than share in the pessimism, I have chosen to address each of these questions in a deliberate, albeit risky effort to identify some possibilities for positive outcomes that would defy the messengers of doom and gloom.

Assessing Mexico's Stability/Instability

It is easy to show that Mexico is potentially more unstable now than it was in the past. The hard part is to estimate Mexico's real prospects for stability/instability.

Never before have there been so many forecasts of impending doom for Mexico's political system—nor so many people, especially right-wing critics, wanting to see such forecasts for one reason or another.[1] Pessimistic assessments challenging the conventional wisdom about the resilience of Mexico's political system and its capacities for control and co-optation mainly come from outside political risk analysts, who are smarting from the Iranian experience and who assess trends by relying on conventional indicator methodologies. They assume that when so many indicators are going badly, something's got to give.

Thus predictions arose that things might "blow up" during mid-1986 when the World Cup soccer matches were held in Mexico, and when elections were held in some Northern Mexican states. But once again Mexico did not blow up. And oddly enough, it could be argued that Mexico's stability during this period was enhanced—not subverted, as so often argued—by the mean-spirited U.S. Congressional hearings held by Senator Jesse Helms during May–June 1986. While these hearings damaged U.S.–Mexican relations by publicly chastising Mexican behavior on various accounts, the repercussions in Mexico led to strong displays of Mexican nationalism in favor of the Mexican government—thereby making it very difficult for anyone, especially from the opposition political parties, to challenge the government without leaving himself open to charges of exhibiting anti-national behavior as a tool of the United States.

Meanwhile, many seasoned experts on Mexico continue to adhere to their conventional analytic faith in Mexico's stability despite its problems. These experts may not be highly optimistic about Mexico's future given current conditions, but because of their experience with the Mexican psyche and the system's resilience they have refrained from embracing those gloomy projections of Mexico as a potential security problem for the United States.

So who is right? I think it boils down to an unclear dialogue between two very different kinds of conventional wisdom.

Whatever the overall strengths and weaknesses of these two analytical approaches to Mexico, the conventional wisdom of the outside risk methodology appears to be terribly flawed regarding Mexican realities. It is thus unlikely to provide a reliable assessment of Mexico's real prospects for stability/instability. Four sets of cautions deserve attention.

The first caution concerns the nature of contradictions in Mexico. That country has always been, and will always be, full of contradictions. Mexicans thrive on contradictions and on dualistic thinking. To them, contradictions do not necessarily mean conflict. I would go so far as to suggest that Mexico is a land of "compatible contradictions." The fact that things are getting worse does not necessarily mean that Mexico is close to collapsing or exploding. The Mexican political–cultural threshold may be much higher than is commonly assumed by standard indicator methodologies. Mexicans know how to accept, tolerate, use, and work with contradictions in ways that North Americans do not understand. For example, U.S. officials and analysts often try to figure out whether Mexico is working with us or against us, but for a Mexican policymaker the most natural and logical course of action may be to do both at the same time.

The second caution has to do with the fact that countries en route to a coup or a revolution may be characterized as going through stages. For example, tensions may yield a crisis, which may yield instability, which may then yield a coup, a revolution, or whatever. In most countries, if things are at one step in this progression, they are not far from being at the next step, and the progression may easily become irreversible. The picture resembles the proverbial "slippery slope." But in Mexico, for reasons we do not understand well, the distance between each step seems to be very long; the overall picture is not one of a slippery slope, but one of a long and winding road across terraced terrain. Mexico can linger at a particular stage for a long time, and, as it waits, something may well come along to halt the progression. Mexico's leaders are specialists at buying time in the face of difficulty. Under such circumstances, the concept of *mañana* may become an asset, not a liability, for stable development.

The reasons for Mexico's inherent resistance to ordinary instability are unclear, but several considerations are worth noting. To begin with, Mexico's political culture is extraordinarily patient and long-suffering, and this helps to sustain a durable nationalism which may be the key to Mexico's political stability. Even when the government appears weak, the Institutional Revolutionary Party (PRI) remains the bastion and chief guardian of this nationalism, and appeals to it may outweigh doubts even about the legitimacy of the political system. Furthermore, many Mexicans believe that the system they now have is the best political option. While the rightist National Action Party (PAN) has posed a minor challenge to the PRI and the government, so far the extreme left has assumed that it could not win a showdown with the government. No other political system in Latin America exhibits this combination of a patient political culture, a fierce and cohesive nationalism, and a perceived absence of better options.

The third caution has to do with the relative importance of internal and external factors in making forecasts about Mexico. The most pessimistic forecasts rely mainly on internal indicators—many of which have looked grim in terms of the long run anyway. Yet, the external factors may be the most decisive. They are also the most difficult to predict. To be sure, internal problems make Mexico more vulnerable to external shocks. Still, what prompted the current concerns about Mexico were largely three external shocks—the fall in the world oil price, the recession in the U.S. economy, and the intensification of conflict in Central America. So it may well be some positive external development (possibly regarding the debt) that will suddenly give Mexico new breathing space, at least for a few years. After all, it does not mean much to say that Mexico may collapse within ten years when such forecasts could have been made many times during the past 50 years.

The fourth caution is that Mexico is the scene not only of multiple crises, but also of multiple struggles (*luchas*) involving the country's top elites and institutions—struggles that would exist even if there were no sense of crisis. These *luchas* revolve around the power of key leaders within the political elite, the state's role in the economy, the federal government's centralized control over northern Mexico, the modernization (but probably not much more democratization) of the PRI and the political party system, and Mexico's participation in the international economy. More broadly, the *luchas* may concern the definition of "the national project," a concept that emerged in the 1970s to refer to the set of integrated long-range policies, plans, and strategies that is, or should be, guiding the Mexican government's efforts to develop a modern nation in keeping with the established principles of Mexican nationalism. Leaders of these *luchas* may at times use, even enhance, the sense of crisis in Mexico for domestic and foreign policy purposes as well as for personal purposes. To outsiders, it may then appear that Mexico is "at the brink"—and it may well be. Yet Mexico may also be far from actually going over the brink because the leaders have carefully orchestrated the game they are playing.

In light of these four sets of cautions, it remains advisable to be skeptical about doomsday forecasts that portend grave instability or a collapse of the Mexican political system. There may be manageable episodes of unrest—the military may even be drawn in to help civilian leaders deal with some specific national security problems—but that is not the same as saying the system will collapse.

A Sea Change in the Political Elite?

Assuming that Mexico remains fairly stable, there is still great uncertainty as to whether the political system—structured much as it has been for the last 50 years—will remain viable or whether it will undergo a transformation. To assess the viability of the political system, one needs to know a good deal more about both the system's institutions and its elites. Yet despite extensive speculation about institutional problems facing the PRI and the presidency, about the need for institutional reforms in favor of democratization and decentralization, and about trends in the composition of the political elite, as well as about the roles and personalities of key leaders—especially now that a change in administration is looming—remarkably little is known about institutional change and the evolution of the political elite in Mexico.

This brief paper cannot remedy that lack of knowledge. Instead, partly on the assumption that the viability of the Mexican political system will turn more on the performance of its elites than its institutions, I will offer yet another optimistic speculation about current and future trends in the development of the political elite.

Since at least the 1930s, the concept of the "revolutionary family" has served to describe Mexico's ruling elite, its composition and structure.[2] One of its great strengths was the ability to include and obtain cooperation from the wide range of personalities, interests, sectors, and ideological tendencies that emerged in the post-Revolutionary period and made some effective claim on political and economic power, demanding a voice as to who should govern Mexico, what the policies should be, and how the benefits should be distributed. As this broadly inclusive elite family developed, it achieved a remarkable degree of cohesion despite the inherent diversity of its membership—a cohesion that rested in large part on the shared principles of balance and equilibrium, and that was thought to involve a "pendulum" whereby different "wings" of the elite would take turns alternating in power across presidential terms.

In its classic form, the revolutionary family became renowned during the 1950s and 1960s for its most prominent wings, the so-called Cardenista and Alemanista wings. These wings, named after former Presidents Lázaro Cárdenas (1934–1940) and Miguel Alemán (1946–1952), came to represent the dominant tendencies within the elite family—the former being more identified with left-of-center, statist, centralist, and nationalist positions, the latter more with right-of-center, conservative, federalist, and pro-private sector positions.[3]

The term "revolutionary family" is still used rhetorically in Mexico to refer to the governing elite. But from an analytical standpoint, so many changes have occurred that this family no longer exists in its classic form. As research by Roderic Camp, Peter Smith and others has shown, major shifts have occurred in the background and recruitment of the political leadership since the late 1960s: from an elite dominated by *politicos* to one dominated by *técnicos*; from an elite where service in and to the PRI was a requirement for ascendance to an elite whose leaders have risen instead by way of service in the government's administrative apparatus; from an elite comprised of regional representatives to an elite recruited mostly from Mexico City; from an elite that included a broad spectrum of representatives, from both the private and the public sectors, to an elite marked by a breach between the two sectors. These shifts took hold in the early 1970s when President Luis Echeverría (1970–1976) ignored stalwarts whose turn it would normally have been to gain high office, and catapulted into his administration numerous young leaders who had supported the massive student-based struggles against the government in 1968.

These shifts have been dramatic. There is still a strong sense of "family" and elite continuity has not been terribly disrupted, in part because many rising stars during the administrations of Presidents Jóse López Portillo (1976–1982) and Miguel de la Madrid (1982–1988) have turned out to be the children of leaders who were prominent in the revolutionary family during the 1930s–1960s. But overall the shifts are substantial enough to provide grist for speculation that a generational sea-change is occurring not only in the background but also in the overall structure and orientation of the elite.

A new elite family appears to be taking shape as the evolutionary successor to the classic revolutionary family. For want of a better term, I will call it the new "institutional family"—a term borrowed from the earlier shift in Mexican politics from a "revolutionary party" during in the 1920s–1930s (the National Revolutionary Party—PNR) to an "institutionalized party" since then (the PRI). The new generation of elites who are gradually forming this institutional family tend to be highly educated, very nationalistic, and, so far, usually left of center and statist in orientation—attributes, incidentally, evinced by many political technocrats. Since the early 1970s, this new generation has gained a strong presence in the central government, and appears to be seeking and gaining influence over the PRI, Congress, and some state governments as the next targets.

Overall, this newly evolving family appears to have a relatively narrow, left-of-center base. There is a substantial conservative wing to the political elite, notably in the PRI; and some Mexican analysts would argue that the key right-wing leaders are more powerful than the leftist–nationalist ones. That may well be true of individual leaders. Nonetheless, the philosophical and political redefinition of the elite family since the 1970s has been motivated if not dominated mainly by the newer left-of-center elements. This has been evident, for example, in the terms of the "national project" as defined during the past ten years.

If this speculation is correct about a sea-change occurring in the elite family, then the key to Mexico's future may lie in what happens to the principle of balance and equilibrium inherent in the old elite concept. At present, balance and equilibrium seem to be lacking among the constituent elements of the new family. For example, terrible breaches exist between those who support a strong public sector and the proponents of a larger role for the private sector.

Compared to the old revolutionary family, then, the new institutional family might be said to have a strong "post-Cardenista" tendency, but to lack a strong "post-Alemanista" tendency. (Here is a further mark of change: "wings" are said to no longer exist, only "tendencies" that are less well defined.) If the new institutional family is to develop as a truly well-integrated, broad-based elite family in keeping with Mexico's pragmatic, time-tested principles of balance and equilibrium, it would not only have to continue consolidating a post-Cardenista wing, but would also have to begin consolidating a well-defined conservative wing, and seek to bridge the two.

Ultimately, that may require a right-of-center leader to accede to the role of president. High-ranking leaders who could fulfill this role and/ or help consolidate a conservative wing reportedly exist, and middle-level leaders who would support such a change are reportedly scattered throughout the political system. In addition, potential political cadres may be found among a young generation of relatively conservative elites who are emerging from some of Mexico's best private schools and private-sector institutions.[4]

But is there evidence that Mexican politics will move in this direction in the near future? To complete the comparison of the old and new elites, President de la Madrid would have to correspond to former President Avila Camacho (1940–1946). In the old elite family, the Cardenista wing was formed first, and the Alemanista wing was created after Avila Camacho, a relative centrist and transitional leader, named Miguel Aleman as his successor. If de la Madrid were to play a similar swing role in naming his successor, he could help broaden the new elite family—assuming a relatively conservative president would, for pragmatic reasons, emphasize elite cohesion despite the bitter animosity between some statist and private-sector elites. But if de la Madrid's successor should turn out to pursue relatively leftist, nationalist, statist policies, then it is likely that the existing, generally left-of-center constituents of the new institutional family may be able to consolidate an exclusive, narrow hold (assuming they do not fight irreconcilably among themselves).

In fact, de la Madrid has named his successor: Carlos Salinas de Gortari. It is far too soon to tell whether Salinas and his administration will develop in what I have called a post-Cardenista or a post-Alemanista direction. Material may be found in his background to suggest either possibility. Or he may move in directions that bear little connection to past tendencies. In any case, the lack of support for his nomination in some PRI-related labor and political circles, and the disagreements about future policy directions that reportedly exist within his transition team, meanwhile suggest that the maintenance of elite cohesion is going to be a significant challenge.

These speculations are offered solely for discussion purposes. Many of my Mexican colleagues would probably question the hypotheses as well as the propriety of a North American making such speculations about the nature of Mexico's political elite. Even so, there is no question that Mexico's elite is changing profoundly, and that the outcome will have substantial implications for Mexico's policies, its political stability, and for U.S.–Mexican relations. What I find "out of whack" politically in Mexico at present is not so much the institutional structure, but rather the elite structure, which is unusually fragmented and fraught with dissension. There may be good reasons to focus on the need for institutional reforms and changes—the usual recommendations about making the PRI and the party system more democratic—but I believe that the key to Mexico's future lies in the structure, composition, and cohesion of its elites. From the perspective of U.S. interests, it is surely more important for the elite structure to evolve in directions consistent with Mexico's own traditional principles of balance and equilibrium, than for reform of the institutional structure to meet certain external (i.e., U.S.) criteria of democracy.

The Military and National Security

Against this background, new questions have also arisen about one of the great mysteries of modern Mexico: the military. These questions derive in part from false rumors that circulated in 1968, 1977, and 1982 about a military coup. The army, though reputed to be one of the most depoliticized in Latin America, has long played a low-profile, residual political role, especially in political intelligence, communications, and control. In recent years, the military as a whole has become visibly more professional and modern, and schools have been created to provide the senior officer corps with advanced training in national security, foreign policy, political, economic, and social, as well as strictly military matters. Is the military now likely to expand its political role? If so, how and where will this show up?

Such questions are difficult to address largely because the Mexican military is more hermetic than any of its counterparts in Latin America. The probability that the military will turn into a disruptive "wild card" for the political system is low; no analyst who has looked at the Mexican military expects it to usurp civilian authority and seek power through a coup. Nonetheless, the military appears to be gradually moving (or being drawn) beyond its residual role in politics, so that the institution and selected officers may play somewhat stronger roles in both making and implementing policies in selected areas. It may thus be more accurate to talk about the military's role in the state than in politics per se.[5]

Military policy does not appear to be the source of any serious political or partisan issues. The military has accepted that Mexico has higher development priorities than the military, and only needs a military with limited capabilities.[6]

Meanwhile, in a country where the very term "national security" has rarely been voiced, national security policy has emerged as an important issue against the background of the riots of 1968, the anti-guerrilla and counter-terrorist operations of the 1970s, the antinarcotics campaigns of the last two decades, and concerns about the security of Mexico's giant oil fields in the late 1970s. National security concerns rose to the fore in this decade following a series of problems along the border with Guatemala, internal debates about the repercussions of the conflict in Central America, and concern about Mexico's own stability. The topic may also have come to the fore because so many people—foreigners for the most part—began warning that Mexico should be concerned about its security.

Defining a national security policy is not seen as a responsibility that should lie primarily with the military. Conceptual development is reportedly controlled by civilian officials who consult with selected military officers. As a result, the concept of national security will be laden with political, social, and economic content.

Although Mexico's concept may necessarily focus on internal security issues, it could acquire a foreign policy content that links Mexico to an emerging Latin American movement for the creation of a regional security system independent of the United States. Collective security and military relations in the Western hemisphere have traditionally been constructed around a pan-American concept—what might be termed a "One Americas" concept—that encompasses the United States and Latin America as a whole, and that has resulted in such shining achievements as the Organization of American States and the Rio Treaty. Mexico has steadfastly kept its distance from this security concept, and from participating in inter-American military activities. Instead, Mexico has sympathized with political/intellectual trends that have been developing in Latin America since the early 1980s, with roots going back decades earlier, to build regional security concepts and mechanisms without direct U.S. participation.

One long-range concept aspires to create an integrated Latin American system that is quite independent of, if not separate from, the United States—what might be termed "Two Americas"—on grounds that the Latin American countries (especially the Spanish-speaking ones) share cultural values, national interests, and political needs different from those of the colossus to the north. In highly nationalistic versions, the United States may be viewed more as a threat than as an ally in the region.

Another, perhaps more pragmatic, concept emphasizes the distinctiveness of different sub-regions (e.g., Central America, the Eastern Caribbean, South America) and favors letting ad-hoc, sub-regional mechanisms arise to take the lead in solving local security problems. This concept—"Many Americas"—seems to contain the greatest ambivalence of the three toward the United States; its proponents may aim to work independently and constrain U.S. power, but at the same time they may also want to engage U.S. cooperation and avoid hostility toward it.

Mexico's political elite appears to be sympathetic to these emerging concepts, as manifested by Mexico's roles in the Latin American Economic System (SELA) since the mid 1970s, the Contadora Group since the early 1980s, and most recently in Latin America's Group of Eight. Since the "One Americas" vision preferred by the United States has steadily lost ground since the mid 1970s, the low-profile struggle developing among these three rival visions of collective security in the Western hemisphere may prove a key concern for U.S. policy during the late 1980s and early 1990s—with Mexico a potentially key player in those concerns.

Whatever direction Mexico ultimately takes, its overall concept of national security will no doubt be consistent with the traditions of Mexican nationalism and the development of the "national project." This is language that the PRI and the president control. Thus, there is little reason to expect that the final concept will mean much in the way of role expansion for the military beyond its clearly assigned responsibilities, which include antinarcotics, antiguerrilla, counter-terrorist, civil order, and border control operations. It has long been rumored that one outcome might be the establishment of a national security council, with the military as one of its members. This would confirm the emergence of the military as a respected and needed actor, and it could provide the officer corps with greater access and influence among the political elite. Yet even then it may not be clear whether the military's role has been enhanced or contained.

Every political–military connection, formal or informal, that surfaces may look like increased military influence in politics. But no institution in Mexico is allowed to develop and modernize without increasingly becoming a partner of the state and the PRI. Hence. political–military connections may be a sign of modernization and institutionalization within Mexico's corporatist system, and of the system's ability to preserve itself through stressful times, without signifying that the military has gained influence at the expense of the civilian leadership.

Mexican Nationalism and U.S.–Mexican Relations

Assuming that the preceding effort at optimism is warranted, the good news is that Mexico may well remain stable and its political system viable for the foreseeable future—especially if the political elite regains its historic balance and cohesion. But along with the good news for U.S. interests comes some unwelcome news for U.S. policy.

An unbreakable thread, the thread of Mexican nationalism, runs through all the preceding good news and helps make it possible. Nationalism is a key force binding the Mexican system together, and keeping its elites and institutions from flying apart in stressful times. Indeed, stress and the task of holding things together in the face of internal and external pressures tend to strengthen nationalism. But because, for deeply rooted historical and cultural reasons, Mexican nationalism, in its rawest form, is often antithetical and rarely hospitable toward the United States, rougher than usual times may lie ahead for U.S.–Mexican relations—even though nationalism will continue to be tempered by Mexican pragmatism, another crucial binding force in the Mexican system.

The nationalist mind-set in Mexico (as elsewhere) revolves around a set of core principles: national dignity, political sovereignty, and economic independence. Adherents to these principles are extremely sensitive to the overbearing presence of the United States, and resent dependency on it. As a result, most analyses of U.S.–Mexican relations by Mexicans and American academics start from observations about the gross asymmetry of power. In keeping with nationalist sensitivities, the logic of asymmetry leads inexorably to a doctrine of diversification—the development of relations with other countries in an effort to balance, if not move away from, close relations with the United Sates.

Asymmetry of power is a fact of life, and any analysis must recognize it. At the same time, the nationalist logic of asymmetry, which is inherently hostile to the growth of U.S.–Mexican relations, runs contrary to the fact that those relations are bound to grow as the two societies and economies become ever more interconnected. What may be needed is another principle, another logic, to address another fact of life: Mexicans hold separate and different views about the "quality" of U.S. attention and the "quantity" of U.S. power. Even when Mexicans complain about the asymmetry of power, they do not want the United States to neglect Mexico; paying less attention to Mexico or to relations with Mexico is not viewed as the way to redress the asymmetry of power. Instead, Mexicans often ask the United States to pay closer attention and to behave more responsibly toward Mexico. Likewise, U.S. criticisms of Mexican policies often boil down to appeals for more responsible behavior.

This line of analysis suggests that the "responsibility of power"— the qualitative effort a nation makes to use its power to attend to another—may deserve to be included alongside the "asymmetry of power" in conceptual frameworks and in policy discussions about bilateral relations. Structural relations may depend heavily on the asymmetry of power, but policy processes and outcomes may depend more on the responsibility of power. Thus, the asymmetry may be acceptable so long as both nations act responsibly—assuming some agreement exists on what being responsible means.

Unlike analyses that emphasize asymmetry, analyses that emphasize mutual responsibility as well as asymmetry in the context of growing interdependence might well conclude that the two countries should rebuild a "special relationship" despite the centrifugal forces of nationalism. Indeed, I would have wished to conclude by saying the times are ripe for a new special relationship. But this does not look like a practical idea for the immediate future, largely because of the effects that global, regional, and domestic conditions have had on the nationalist thinking Mexicans and Americans engage in about each other.

In the United States, Mexico is perceived (and misperceived) as being internally weak, fragile, and adrift; as having a foreign policy that creates problems for U.S. interests in Central America; and as becoming potentially vulnerable to meddling by external radical actors. Such perceptions are dangerous in that they may lead to a nationalist wish to exert pressure on Mexico according to a "now that they are down, let's get 'em and make 'em shape up" kind of thinking.

In Mexico, meanwhile, the United States is increasingly perceived (and misperceived) as an unprincipled, indecisive superpower in domestic disarray. The sight of U.S. power beleaguered and declining in a perilous world does not arouse much sympathy or dismay in Mexico. On the contrary, such perceptions may fuel the nationalist wish to take initiatives that display Mexico's independence and create distance, according to a "now that they are down, let's get away" kind of thinking.[7]

There is no easy way out of the dilemmas posed by the worsening nationalist perceptions each country has of the other. Should these perceptions prevail, they will invite mutual recrimination and expectation of the worst kind of behavior from each other. Presumably they will not prevail when it really matters, thus allowing Mexico and the United States to muddle through to better times.

Notes

1. For sophisticated pessimism, see Brian Latell, *Mexico at the Crossroads: The Many Crises of the Political System,* The Hoover Institution, Stanford University, June 16, 1986.
2. The classic description is in Frank R. Brandenburg, *The Making of Modern Mexico,* Prentice-Hall, Englewood Cliffs, New Jersey, 1964.
3. I use the terms "left" and "right," and later "post-Cardenista" and "'post-Alemanista" with some trepidation. Of course, moving left or right are not

necessarily the only criteria or options. In addition, an analyst must always be aware that political *camarillas* (cliques) built around strong leaders in Mexico often contain members whose diversity of political and economic orientations do not lend themselves to easy or uniform categorization. Indeed, it can be advantageous for a *camarilla* to include members from diverse ideological and other sectors, some of which may on the surface appear to be in contradiction or competition with each other.

4. On this last point, see the articles by Daniel Levy and Peter Smith in Roderic A. Camp, *Mexico's Political Stability: The Next Five Years*, Westview Press, Boulder, Colorado, 1986.

5. A spectrum of views appears in Ronfeldt, ed., *The Modern Mexican Military: A Reassessment*, Monograph Series, 13, Center for U.S.–Mexican Studies, University of California at San Diego, La Jolla, 1984.

6. Optimism aside, there is an operational question as to whether the military, with its limited capabilities, could handle serious episodes of violent unrest, were they to occur. The military has adequate capabilities to handle instability in Mexico City so long as the provinces are quiet—and vice versa—and it could handle serious unrest at the mass level so long as elite cohesion and integration remain strong. But the military may not have adequate capabilities to handle a crisis occurring simultaneously in Mexico City and the provinces that cuts across both elite and mass lines of struggle.

7. If such a pattern of behavior were to take hold in Mexico, U.S. analysts might have to worry about Mexico becoming openly anti-American and playing "the Soviet card" in its foreign relations. This is unlikely to occur under present circumstances; Mexico has fended off recent Soviet overtures to open new consular offices (e.g., in Northern Mexico close to the U.S. border) and obtain permission for port visits by Soviet naval units. But under conditions of exacerbated nationalism, the possibility of Mexico playing "the Soviet card" could arise in the future, notably if the Sandinistas consolidate a pro-Soviet, Marxist–Leninist regime in Nicaragua. Many Mexican nationalists believe that the Cuban revolution and the Soviet presence there somehow increase the "degrees of freedom" that Mexico has to act independently of the United States—a logic that now apparently applies as well to some Mexican views of the Nicaraguan revolution.

Part III
Immigration

U.S. Immigration Reform: A Mexican Perspective

Jorge A. Bustamante

Undocumented immigration from Mexico to the United States reflects supply and demand. The U.S. needs foreign labor, while Mexico has a surplus of labor. In the past, Mexico favored such migration, regarding it as an "escape valve" from pressures generated by high rates of unemployment. Now that the migrant population includes workers in services and industry, as well as in agriculture, Mexico considers such migration a drain on its labor force. Mexico therefore seeks bilateral discussions to protect the labor and human rights of its workers in the United States. The United States, however, regards the issue as one of law enforcement, which leads it to act unilaterally. To encourage the United States to deal with migration bilaterally, Mexico should tie future negotiations over the debt issue to a U.S. willingness to negotiate over immigration.

THE U.S.–MEXICO BORDER has many openings. These openings serve not only as conduits for people migrating north, but as channels for the movement of many nonhuman goods and substances in many directions and for many reasons. Undocumented migrants are the most conspicuous users of the porous border. But the border also provides a pathway for undocumented capital flight from Mexico, undocumented natural resources that are escaping underground and through aquatic routes, and undocumented contaminants originating on both sides of the border that are polluting our international environment. There are also risks inherent to life on the border that transcend the geographic boundary itself, such as Mexico's sharing of effects of a nuclear holocaust with a U.S. target close to the border, and the influence of the movement across the border of such abstract concepts as values, ideas, and myths.

It is reasonable and desirable to require that everything that enters our respective countries be recognized and recorded, and that it pass through a controlled gate. The reality of border life, however, dictates something very different. The free will of international neighbors determines supply and demand of labor force, capital, technology, services, and other resources on the basis of mutual satisfaction. This does not mean that this interdependence is always symmetrical. On the contrary, the consequences of interdependence are not always shared on an equal basis by the actors on either side of the border. However, the interdependence exists, and it is an intricate and intrinsic part of the U.S.–Mexico border reality, determined by the goods and services that permeate the border.

This is not to suggest that everything that is transmitted to either country through these border openings is either desirable or beneficial. However, these undocumented flows form part of a complex de facto reality that characterizes the entire border region.

In this paper, I will focus on the problem of undocumented migration from legal, economic, and social perspectives, and I will present an approach to a bilateral solution of the problem.

The Political and Juridical Context of U.S. Immigration Laws

Any comprehensive analysis of undocumented migration from Mexico must begin by developing an understanding of the economic and social context of the openings along the international boundary. A basic premise for this analysis is that every nation has the sovereign right to decide who may enter its territory and who may not. Immigration laws and restrictions derive from this sovereign right. However, when immigration laws are designed to operate as domestic labor supply laws, this right becomes abused. The "Texas proviso" of the McCarran–Walter Act of 1952 is a case in point. This measure, drafted by Texas legislators, made the United States the only country in the world where immigration laws explicitly allowed employers to hire aliens who had entered national territory in violation of those same laws. This provision remained on the books from 1952 until 1986, when it was supplanted by the Simpson–Rodino bill.

By accepting the Texas proviso as part of the law of the land, the U.S. Congress decided to open a door to facilitate the supply of foreign labor for American employers. It can hardly be argued that the United States "has lost control of its borders" when the government itself created a legal channel to promote the cause of the loss—undocumented immigration—as a response to the domestic demand for labor. The U.S. notion that the presence of undocumented Mexican workers in the United States represents a threat to its borders, and to its national sovereignty, conveys the impression that these workers are the enemy of U.S. national integrity. Only a notion so dramatic and so skewed could elicit such powerfully negative reactions to undocumented Mexican workers' presence in the United States.

The reality is something quite different. Historically, undocumented Mexican migrants have contributed substantially and positively to the creation of wealth in the United States. They were not the enemy of war-pressed U.S. industries during World War II. Nor have they been the enemy of agricultural rural development in California or of southwestern railroads.

Moreover, the idea that loss of control of national borders explains the presence of undocumented immigrants from Mexico insinuates that a domestic solution to the problem, or threat, is in order. It also suggests that the nature of the solution be a forceful one, and provides the U.S. Border Patrol as the most logical approach. Therefore, this theory distorts the bilateral nature of undocumented immigration.

Above all, undocumented immigration is a phenomenon that results from the existence of a binational labor market, where the demand from the United States for foreign labor is as real as the supply of it from Mexico. Undocumented migration is therefore a truly bilateral phenomenon, shaped by the interaction of factors originating on both sides of the border.

But it is not a symmetrical interaction, and its asymmetry is due primarily to the current U.S. immigration laws. When the Texas proviso was in effect, U.S. employers had the right to decide whether to treat a Mexican migrant as a worker or as a criminal offender. An act of will by the employer, one as simple as a telephone call to the U.S. Immigration and Naturalization Service (INS), could make the difference. The point is not how many employers in fact exercised that power, but that until very recently, such actions were perfectly legal. In this respect, the Texas provision supplied the legal basis for the asymmetry that has characterized the interdependence between the demands of the U.S. labor force and the economic needs of Mexican migrants.

The Mexican people want to negotiate this asymmetrical interdependence, and we ask the United States to treat the phenomenon of undocumented immigration as a bilateral issue. As a basic premise for these negotiations, we propose that both countries recognize that there are costs and benefits attached to the phenomenon for each, and that costs and benefits alike need to be viewed from a bilateral perspective. The legislative approach taken so far, exemplified by the Texas provision, has not corresponded to the bilateral nature of the phenomenon.

Out-Migration from Mexico and the National Interest

There has been a significant change within the Mexican Government regarding the conceptualization of the out-migration of workers. In the past, the prevalent belief was that the outflow of migrant workers to the United States constituted an "escape valve" and represented a relief from pressures due to unemployment in Mexico. Therefore, the government had an interest in opening or maintaining this escape valve, provided that there was an international agreement under which the flow could be managed.

This was the Mexican Government's view at the time the "*bracero* agreements" ended in 1965.* But the view has gradually changed, as the migratory phenomenon has become more complex and has grown to comprise a broader socioeconomic spectrum of the society, by, among other means, shifting its base from rural to urban populations.

Changes on the supply side have paralleled changes on the demand side. The characteristics of U.S. labor demands have increasingly diversified, shifting from farmwork to services and industry. With growing numbers of Mexican migrant workers having achieved higher levels of education than were typical in the past, the notion of "labor-force drain" has replaced that of safety valve. This shift became evident in the late 1970s and early 1980s, when Mexican and U.S. employers began to compete for the same Mexican work force; the result was an increasing awareness by Mexican employers of the costs of such compensation. The Mexican economic crisis that started in 1982 essentially removed this competition as a significant variable, except in the maquiladora or in-bond industry, but the new awareness of the relation between long-term internal economic development and out-migration to the United States has remained.

The Mexican Senate took the lead in suggesting that planning for internal economic development could not proceed alongside the out-migration of any segment of the labor force. Senator Miguel González Avelar, in his opening remarks to the 22nd Mexico–United States

* In 1942 the United States requested Mexico to cooperate with the Allied war effort by providing needed labor for U.S. agricultural production. The Mexican government agreed to do so, and the first of a series of contractual bilateral labor agreements, or "bracero agreements," was signed. The last agreement ended in 1965.

Interparliamentary Meeting, held in 1984, stated that "in the long run, out-migration from Mexico to the United States is contrary to the national interest." He went on to say that in the short run, it is evident, the Mexican economy cannot absorb all of its working-age population, much less compete with U.S. wages. On the other hand, it would be unconstitutional to implement any kind of police action to prevent either internal or external migration.

These remarks could be interpreted as meaning that the Mexican Government's policy on international migration is geared toward promoting a bilateral discussion and negotiating an agreement with the United States to protect the labor rights and human rights of Mexican workers under U.S. laws and international guidelines. A basic innovation of this approach is that it is not concerned with negotiating quotas of contracted migrant workers. Rather, its goal is to develop a long-term, bilateral legal framework under which U.S.–Mexico interdependence related to the binational labor market can be discussed, while conditions in Mexico are gradually modified to discourage out-migration to the United States. This new approach toward the outflow of migrant workers was made explicit to U.S. senators and congressmen by their Mexican counterparts in the context of the interparliamentary meeting.

So far, the response from the United States has been more of the same. The unilateral U.S. approach, exemplified by internal legislation, was reaffirmed in 1986 with the passage of the Simpson–Rodino bill. From a Mexican perspective, this reform legislation represents a political solution to a politically defined problem. The U.S. Congress has defined the presence of undocumented immigrants as an indication that the country "has lost control of its borders," and it has acted in accordance with that definition, as if the new legislation were going to recover what has supposedly been lost.

The uproar against the Mexican undocumented immigrants that preceded the passage of the bill cooled off long before the new legislation could be technically enforced. In the first week of January 1987, Alan Nelson, commissioner of the INS, was quoted as saying that there had been a decline in apprehensions of undocumented immigrants at the U.S.–Mexico border, and that this was probably due to the passage of the immigration reforms. However, as recently as October 1986, before Congress approved the bill, he had stated, in a joint press conference with Attorney General Edwin Meese, that a "definitive link had been established between illegal aliens and the drug traffic from Mexico." Months earlier, Commissioner Nelson had announced similar "links" between undocumented immigrants from Mexico and the rise of crime in San Diego and other U.S. border cities, and between undocumented migrants and the threat of terrorism.

Assuming that the Simpson–Rodino reform is a political solution, it can be expected to have no significant impact on the actual practices of U.S. hiring of undocumented immigrants from Mexico. The basis for this hypothesis is twofold. First, an almost completely ignored fact in the United States is that 13 states have already amended their labor laws, and no changes have been registered in the practice of hiring undocumented immigrants in those states. Second, the employer sanction provisions of the Simpson–Rodino bill appear so unenforceable as to have little potential effect.

Sanctions against employers do not become fully enforceable until after an 18-month grace period ends in May 1988. Then, to prove compliance, an employer who has hired an undocumented immigrant can simply tell a law enforcer that the worker showed him a driver's license or a passport that appeared to be valid. If the employer produces a record of the notations required by the new law—the name of the worker hired and the type of document provided to prove a legal resident status—the word of the worker weighed against that of the employer will determine whether the alien is charged with use of falsified documents, even if the alien had not shown any document to the employer who hired him.

What the new law was doing, even before it was signed by President Ronald Reagan, was encouraging a mushrooming industry of falsified documents, based on the understanding that the employer is not required by the new legislation to retain a copy of the document or verify its authenticity beyond face value.

On the other hand, the law authorized an unprecedented increase in the INS budget for the purpose of almost doubling the number of officers assigned to patrol the U.S.–Mexico border.

It is the sovereign right of the United States to legislate in whatever way its Congress determines. This same sovereign right supports the existence and operation of the U.S. Border Patrol. The issue for Mexicans is not the nature of the right the United States has as a sovereign nation to act unilaterally; rather, it is that the United States is approaching migration from Mexico in a unilateral fashion, when the issue is inherently a bilateral one, which must be treated as such in order to develop appropriate and effective strategies. We take issue with this unilateral approach, because one country cannot by itself solve the problematic consequences of a phenomenon that intrinsically involves two countries in its origins, its costs, and its benefits. Mexicans are concerned that the unilateral approach favored by the United States on immigration policies will not solve the dilemmas caused by undocumented immigration from Mexico. It will achieve only makeshift and ineffective solutions. We believe that the commitment expressed by many in the United States to curtail the inflow of undocumented immigrants can be effectively served only through a bilateral approach. It bears repeating that Mexico would prefer to export goods, rather than undocumented workers.

In spite of the increasing complexity of bilateral issues, the United States and Mexico share a record of harmonious relations as neighboring countries. Close to 10 million persons live along both sides of the 2,000-mile border. A significant proportion of them interact intensively across that border on a daily basis. Despite cultural diversity and economic disparity, those interactions can very easily be described as amicable. Conflict is not absent, but it is much more the exception than the rule. Moreover, the two countries also share a record of peaceful solutions to bilateral controversies. Together we have responded in a civilized manner to great challenges within our relationship. Precedents exist within U.S.–Mexican relations to suggest that a jointly constructed bilateral approach to questions of transboundary migration would not be new or unrealistic.

The Question of Numbers

A bilateral approach to undocumented immigration would have to be based on reliable data that scientifically measure the costs and benefits of that phenomenon for both sides of the border. There are currently no reliable statistics on the volume of undocumented migrants from Mexico, as is evidenced by the change in official U.S. estimates over a 10-year period. In 1974, INS Commissioner Leonard Chapman stated in Congress that there could be as many as 20 million illegal Mexican aliens in the United States. In 1984, the U.S. Bureau of the Census estimated that there were 2–3 million undocumented immigrants from Mexico. A drop in estimates from 20 million to 2 million in 10 years suggests that there is something wrong with the shaping of the official numbers on undocumented immigrants.

Public opinion in the United States, however, demands quantified descriptions of the extent of the problem. Interestingly, Dr. Celestino Fernández, of the University of Arizona, has demonstrated that a single source is the most dominant in shaping public opinion about the presence of undocumented Mexican workers in the United States. This source is none other than the INS. There are no data available to demonstrate that INS officials do not have accurate information about the number of undocumented immigrants in the United States. However, there is one unequivocal source of misleading information: INS statistics on apprehensions of illegal aliens. These numbers are used as the main empirical basis for arriving at an estimate of their actual number in the United States.

Quotes on INS statistics of apprehensions can be found almost every day in U.S. newspapers. What do not appear are statements explaining that these statistics represent specific events, but not specific individuals. The same individual can be apprehended several times in one year, in one month, and even in one day. Every apprehension is recorded on the books, but statistics do not reflect repeated attempts by the same individual, only the aggregate number of apprehensions. Thus are INS statistics reported to and interpreted by the public.

The American public has also been led to believe that the statistics on apprehensions represent only a small portion of the total volume of undocumented immigration; the statistics are often accompanied by such statements as, "for every one that is caught, 3–5 go unapprehended." What is not explained in the reporting of these statistics is that the number of apprehensions of undocumented aliens might well be a function of the combined factors of the actual volume of the flow and the capabilities of INS officials to apprehend these people.

Estimates of the number of undocumented immigrants in the United States based on such misleading interpretation of data have created confusion in the public mind about the impact of these immigrants on the national scene. A bilateral approach to this question should include a way to clear up this confusion.

Toward a Bilateral Approach

According to the predominant U.S. view, undocumented migration is a criminal problem that is addressable through law enforcement procedures and reform of existing immigration laws. These approaches are by definition unilateral.

In Mexico, by contrast, undocumented migration is seen as the result of a basically economic phenomenon that corresponds to the interaction of supply and demand in the binational labor market. Therefore, Mexico considers undocumented migration a bilateral phenomenon, which necessarily requires bilateral focus, bilateral debate, and bilateral resolution. It views the undocumented migrants as actors in an economic game with rules that are extremely disadvantageous to them. They are able, nevertheless, to glean some advantages, both for themselves and for their sending country, despite the benefits that accrue to their employers and the receiving country. Migrants view themselves, and their communities view them, as a positive element. There is even a degree of pride in being a migrant worker or the close relative of one.

Thus, the very same phenomenon is seen in a generally negative light in the United States and in a generally positive one in Mexico. This contrast leads to the conclusion that resolving the undocumented migration problem would require redefining the issue in terms acceptable to both countries. My feeling, however, is that we cannot wait for the development of such a definition. We must move ahead toward a bilateral negotiation, despite the differing definitions of the problem. I propose an approach that would pull together two bilateral issues: international migration and Mexico's external debt.

Alternative Solution

This proposal derives from several assumptions:

1. Both creditors and debtor countries recognize that the external debt is, at its simplest level, a bilateral issue and, at its most complex level, a multilateral one. That is, no one would suggest that a unilateral focus suffices for resolving foreign debt problems.

2. There is a growing consensus among actors involved in addressing the external debt problem that there is a need to follow new and mutually accepted steps to avoid a scenario in which debtor countries are forced to choose between stimulating economic growth and making payments on their foreign debt.

3. Prevailing public opinion in the United States favors ending undocumented migration.

4. The migration of undocumented Mexicans is viewed in the United States as the result exclusively of forces endogenous to Mexico.

5. In the U.S. view, Mexico's ability to make payment on its external debt and to halt emigration is tied to its ability to reconcile political stability with scarce monetary resources.

6. Political instability in Mexico could augment emigration to the United States and undermine Mexico's ability to address its foreign debt problem.

7. Mexico's opportunities to renegotiate the terms of its external debt payments are, paradoxically, tied to the dimension of that debt.

8. This paradoxical negotiating card can be used to encourage a bilateral approach to both issues—external debt and undocumented migration—to the extent that the United States associates both with Mexico's political stability.

Although Mexicans may not share certain views commonly held in the United States regarding the nature of undocumented migration, they may nevertheless benefit from linking the mutually recognized bilateral nature of the external debt to the unrecognized bilateral nature of undocumented labor migration. All the assumptions can therefore operate as elements in a logical chain that leads to the last two assumptions where both countries can agree that political instability in Mexico is contrary to their respective national interests.

However, even if we accept this logical sequence, we still lack the means for linking negotiation on the external debt to that on undocumented migration. The proposal of a bilateral agreement that would link these two questions rests on the following points:

1. The Mexican Government could reach an accord with the United States to channel a portion of the actual interest owed on the external debt to a fund for the construction in Mexico of a system of labor-intensive agro-industrial productive units designed to attract former or potential migrant workers. The money used to set up this fund would be repaid with the export earnings from the goods produced by the productive units.

2. Given specific quality guarantees, the U.S. Government would accept part of the production from these units to supply its ongoing food relief and food assistance programs.

3. This program would keep migrant workers in Mexico. Its success could be measured by reductions in the flow of undocumented Mexican workers to the United States.

4. Agreement on the amount of financing for the production system and the terms of its operation would be based on the results of a joint binational feasibility study, conducted by reputable scientific research institutions.

This study would specify the following:

(a) The products these units could produce that would be most appropriate for export in terms of the demands of U.S. food assistance programs

(b) Optimal locations for these units in terms both of production and export potential, and of impact on the migratory population

(c) Modes of organizing production in accordance with the first two considerations

(d) Assembly-line methods for producing goods with export potential

(e) The means for financing these units and setting terms for payment in agreement with subsequent terms of servicing the interest of the external debt

5. The time allotted for this binational study would constitute a grace period, during which payment of a portion of the interest on Mexico's foreign debt (the amount mutually agreed upon for financing the system of production units) would be temporarily suspended.

This proposal has the following advantages:

(a) It would unite two principles of Mexican policy with two problems Mexico shares with the United States: to grow in order to pay the debt, and to export products rather than labor.

(b) It would directly address the real and apparent relationships among external debt, political stability, and labor migration to the United States.

(c) It would improve the precarious footing of two bilateral issues presently addressed unilaterally by the U.S. Government: U.S. protectionism, which limits Mexican exports to the U.S., and the persisting U.S. Government resolve to address the issues of undocumented migration through unilateral law enforcement measures.

(d) It would have an anti-inflationary impact, because prices and export schedules for the goods produced by the units would be pre-established.

(e) The operation of the system could be modified depending on its impact on the servicing of the debt, and on any decrease in the migratory flow to the United States.

Buttressing this proposal is the vast amount of information the Mexican Senate collected during the open hearings on labor migration that it conducted throughout 1985. This information and analysis, presented by Mexico's preeminent researchers in the field of migration, highlight the urgent need to reinforce the premise presented by the Mexican Senate that a national development plan cannot proceed in the face of the continuous emigration of the country's labor force. Within this premise lies one of the conclusions of these open hearings: that over the long term, the emigration of Mexican workers to the United States runs counter to Mexico's national interests. The same forum also yielded the consensus that the Mexican Government's immediate objectives relating to undocumented migration should be, first, to protect the human and labor rights of Mexican migrant workers in the United States, and, second, to negotiate bilaterally their working and residence conditions in the United States, in order to guarantee both labor and human rights.

Undocumented migration to the United States constitutes a problem for Mexicans because of the unequal relationship it establishes between the Mexican worker and his U.S. employer. U.S. society labels these workers "illegal aliens," a term that downplays the benefits the United

States receives from this readily available labor force. The undocumented workers who cultivate California's fields and orchards are not criminals. Neither are the undocumented women who bring their labor and their strong belief in a closely knit family to the care of American children, whose parents are thus able to seek more attractive employment opportunities and to increase their family income. Undocumented Mexicans who, through their taxes and their contributions to the social security system, support public services and U.S. workers' retirement funds, are not criminals. They are actors in a de facto and asymmetrical phenomenon of interdependence that is in urgent need of rational management.

The border between the United States and Mexico divides and unites. It divides, because it marks the beginning and the end of our national identities, which we want to preserve. It unites, because all of us, on both sides, realize that only by learning to reach across it and working together can we pursue happiness with equality and freedom.

A Bilateral Approach to Migration Control?

Manuel García y Griego

Because a large proportion of undocumented migration originates in Mexico, some policy analysts advocate a bilateral approach to its control. Such an approach, however, may be difficult and even undesirable. Within the United States, international migration is viewed as a domestic law enforcement problem that also involves the sovereign right of the United States to decide whether to admit aliens. Mexico also does not regard migration as a subject for bilateral negotiation, but for different reasons. People in both the United States and Mexico who advocate a bilateral approach to migration control ignore the fact that the two countries have fundamental differences in national objectives.

ON NOVEMBER 6, 1986, President Ronald Reagan signed into law the Immigration Reform and Control Act (IRCA), also known as the Simpson–Rodino bill. This complex legislation seeks to reduce the number of illegal entries into the United States and, especially, the number of undocumented aliens already living in the United States. Of the nearly four million undocumented persons residing or working temporarily in the United States, approximately 2.5 million are Mexicans. As a result, the legislation potentially affects Mexico more than it does any other country outside the United States.

In part because such a large proportion of the undocumented migration has originated in Mexico, in recent years some policy analysts have advocated a bilateral approach to migration control, either as an alternative to IRCA or as a necessary complement to it. These arguments, however, have not recognized that there are large political obstacles to U.S.–Mexican control over northward migration. A bilateral approach would not only be difficult to devise, but, given the prevailing definitions of national interests regarding migration issues in both countries, it may be undesirable.

Control has two major empirical components: government control over the number of migrants and over their immigration status in the United States. When the United States adopted IRCA, it had both aspects in mind; its goals are to reduce future undocumented migration and to legalize certain undocumented migrants already in the country. In Mexico, large-scale emigration is also seen as undesirable, though for different reasons; nevertheless, Mexico recognizes that for the foreseeable future, emigration in one form or another will be a necessary evil. Mexicans place greater emphasis on the issue of the immigration status of migrants than on their number, preferring that their fellow citizens in the United States be there legally.

The immigration reform adopted in 1986 ends the discussion, perhaps for several years, about whether the United States should pursue bilateral agreements with Mexico and other sending countries as an *alternative* to domestic legislation. If bilateral agreements are reached, they will be adjuncts to, and not substitutes for, IRCA. Post–Simpson-Rodino bilateral cooperation, however, is not moot. Though this was not widely publicized, in December 1986, President Miguel de la Madrid was consulted by the U.S. Commissioner of Immigration regarding the potential effects of the legislation in Mexico. The Act mandates two other consultations with Mexico: the solicitation of Mexican views on the somewhat modified provisions for recruiting temporary agricultural workers (the so-called H-2A program); and one of the commissions established by IRCA is charged, during its three-year lifetime, with consulting with sending countries regarding emigration and international economic cooperation.

The effectiveness of the unilateral U.S. attempt to achieve some degree of migration control is, as yet, untested. However, there is reason to doubt the efficacy of the employer sanctions prescribed in the 1986 Act. This view is based on skepticism that employer sanctions are an effective migration control measure, but it is also based on the consideration that *any* measure adopted by the United States in the near term would probably be inadequate in the face of likely future migration pressures. On the one hand, during the coming decade, Mexico's economic growth is expected to be too anemic to absorb many new workers, yet the population of individuals of labor-force age will be growing at about 3.5 percent annually. On the other hand, the United States is expected to suffer a shortage of unskilled workers, even though estimates of the magnitude of the shortage are imprecise. For some years now, students of "labor-market interdependence" have interpreted this situation to mean that both countries would benefit if they encouraged and managed increased labor flows from Mexico to the United States. Though IRCA may deter undocumented migration somewhat, it seems likely to persist in smaller numbers over the medium term.

The advantages of U.S.–Mexican management of northward labor migration for either country are not obvious, nor is it my purpose to discuss what these advantages might be. Instead, I focus on past and continuing political obstacles to bilateral approaches that might address the problem of migration control. These obstacles are deeply embedded in the domestic politics of each country, and the differences between the two governments regarding migration control pose problems whose resolutions are matters not merely of goodwill.

Domestic Obstacles to Bilateral Cooperation

The U.S. Government and American society as a whole perceive international migration as a domestic issue, which should be discussed in the arena of national politics and dealt with through policies formulated by Congress. In practice, this perception translates into a bias toward a unilateral approach. Despite the obvious international repercussions of immigration policy-making, the United States is not prepared to deal with the subject as a foreign policy matter. Congress reflects this thinking in the way it assigns legislative jurisdiction: Immigration legislation is lodged principally with the judiciary committees of both houses, and the foreign affairs committees have little, if anything, to do with the subject. Within the executive branch, despite operational responsibilities in the issuance of visas by U.S. consulates, it is the Justice Department—not State—that is responsible for immigration policy-making.

The reasons why the issue is considered a domestic matter can be explored both at the level of U.S. political elites, where the policy problem is most clearly defined and articulated, and at the level of U.S. public opinion, which largely supports this definition. There seem to be different elements that explain why political elites in the United States consider this a domestic matter: First, the undocumented immigration issue is viewed as a law enforcement problem. Second, the decision of whether to admit foreigners, and under what conditions, is considered a sovereign right. Finally, the problem is characterized by a strong element of inertia—that is, it has essentially been viewed as a domestic matter during the century or so that the federal government has assumed direct control over immigration policy, and it continues to be viewed that way.

Public opinion reflects similar attitudes. The U.S. public is apparently convinced that the country "has lost control of its borders." Control in this sense is a unilateral concept, not something that is negotiable. The admission of immigrants, moreover, is by and large conceived as a matter of permanently admitting new members to

American society. And in principle, the decision of a community to invite or reject new members is a nonnegotiable issue. Finally, the U.S. public, like the political elites, has grown accustomed to thinking of immigration in domestic policy terms; over time, it has come to associate immigration issues with debates over job competition, use of public services, law enforcement problems, bilingual education, and changes in the ethnic composition of neighborhoods. At both the elite and the popular levels, then, little attention has been paid to the consequences of immigration policy on the immigrants' countries of origin or on U.S. relations with those countries. The legislative process of the past years, whose result was IRCA, has been faithful to these attitudes.

The extent of the U.S. commitment to a unilateral approach is illustrated by the failure of the U.S. immigration debate to focus on the potential consequences of current proposals on countries of origin. For example, there is a widespread U.S. perception that emigration relieves Mexico of employment pressures, and that the reduction of migration would close a "safety valve." Without that valve, according to this view, Mexico's economy, and possibly its political system, would experience severe pressure, particularly under present circumstances. However, this view, and more apocalyptic views of what might happen to Mexico if migration were to be reduced, did not carry sufficient weight, in congressional or public debates, to persuade Congress to explore either a unilateral alternative, potentially more acceptable and less harmful to Mexico, or a bilateral approach before adopting control legislation. Given the perception that U.S. action might adversely affect Mexico and that such negative effects could boomerang on the United States, public support for strong measures to reduce undocumented immigration indicates a remarkable predisposition toward unilateral action.

This formidable bias, however, reflects not only traditional U.S. attitudes toward immigration policy, but also an indifference to the external consequences of such policies due to the asymmetry of power between the United States and the countries of origin. The unilateral bias is sustained by political realities: The United States is in a position to ignore international public opinion, as well as the external costs of its immigration policies. Whatever their merits, Simpson–Rodino and its predecessors were framed the way they were because domestic public opinion was all that mattered. Since the United States has not been forced by circumstances to face the short-term external costs of domestically focused policies, it has had little incentive to view immigration policy-making in other terms.

The previous considerations might appear to suggest that because of inertia, deeply held attitudes, and political realities, the United States cannot consider immigration a negotiable matter. This is not exactly true. A more accurate conclusion is that from the U.S. point of view, the political basis for negotiation is quite narrow. Immigration, in some sense, apparently is negotiable. However, to the extent that the U.S. objective is to rid itself of certain undesirable nationals by obtaining the cooperation of their governments, the political basis for bilateral agreement is rather narrow. A number of examples illustrate this point.

After Congress enacted the Chinese Exclusion Act of 1882, U.S. national sentiment favored a similar exclusion of Japanese immigrants. To accomplish the same goal without enacting legislation, the United States in 1907 negotiated a gentlemen's agreement with Japan in which the Japanese Government agreed not to issue passports to most of its nationals seeking admission to the United States. The United States eventually broke its end of the bargain and excluded all Japanese immigrants in 1924. More recently, the United States and Cuba have reached agreements—which have ultimately fallen through—to send back Cuban inmates in U.S. detention centers who arrived illegally in the United States during the 1980 Mariel boatlift. Similarly, in 1982 the United States successfully obtained Haitian government cooperation in the sea interdiction of emigrants fleeing Haiti for the United States. In each of these instances, a particular component of immigration was viewed as a *cost* to the United States, and cooperation was sought from foreign governments in reducing emigration flows or accepting the return of undesirable aliens.

There is one major historical exception to this pattern: the *bracero* program, a series of bilateral agreements spanning two decades that provided for joint control of the migration and terms of employment of Mexican laborers in the United States. Despite its longevity, however, the *bracero*, or agricultural workers, program was an aberration in U.S. immigration policy—indeed, it is frequently not considered part of immigration policy at all. The birth of this bilateral experiment, in 1942, was made possible by the extraordinary circumstances of U.S. entry into World War II, Mexican cooperation with the war effort, the U.S. Good Neighbor Policy, and a strong Mexican bargaining position vis-à-vis the United States. The continuation of the program for nearly two decades after World War II was the result of somewhat less unusual, but nevertheless favorable, circumstances: the predominance of the view in the United States that American national interests were served by its continuation, the Mexican concessions that reduced the effectiveness of the labor guarantees, the peculiarities of U.S. agricultural politics, and the fact that the negotiation involved *nonimmigrant* workers. To be sure, the United States and Mexico agreed to reduce illegal entries into the United States as part of the *bracero* bargain, but their agreement did not detract from the basic premise that both countries gained from the migration of Mexican workers. In the early 1960s, when that premise was no longer accepted in the United States, the program was terminated unilaterally.

To the extent that the overriding U.S. interest of reducing emigration to the United States continues to reflect past perceptions, the experiences of the *bracero* program would appear to have little relevance to future bilateral discussion, and the political basis in the United States for bilateral agreement is likely to remain narrow.

The Mexican Government is not disposed to regard migration as a subject for negotiation either, but for different reasons. Indeed, the idea of international migration agreements has great appeal in Mexico; if there is a Mexican bias, it runs in a direction opposite to that of the United States. In some quarters, the predisposition toward a bilateral approach is so strong, that it even denies the legitimacy of unilateral action.

Mexico is unprepared to negotiate matters of emigration control because the domestic political costs of addressing the subject are high. One reason for this sensitivity is the treatment that Mexican migrants receive in the United States at the hands of employers, local governments, and federal officers. Another reason is what the Mexican Government is doing—or not doing—about it. Over the past few years, the Mexican Government has improved to a significant degree the extent and quality of consular protection afforded to its nationals, but it obviously could do more. The likelihood that Mexican diplomacy can significantly reduce the number and seriousness of border shootings and other incidents, however, does not appear to be high. At this time, there is the perception that there is little that the Mexican Government can do to reduce the mistreatment of Mexicans in the United States. Consequently, such incidents are likely to continue to be irritants in Mexican domestic policies and in bilateral relations.

In other respects as well, emigration is a no-win issue in Mexico. Public opinion lays a good part of the blame for emigration on the shortcomings of Mexican economic policies, past and present. Such policies are not blameless, of course, nor is there any doubt that at the level of individual migrants, poverty and underemployment at home are strong incentives for emigration. However, it is far from self-evident that different economic policies would significantly alter emigration flows. Economic hardship is widespread in Mexico, and is not limited to the relatively small number of Mexicans who actually migrate. The geographic distribution of the sources of this migration has been remarkably stable over several decades, and it bears little or no resemblance to the geographic distribution of poverty or marginalization in Mexico. The states from which three-fourths of the migrants originate are not the poorest in the country; the same would probably hold true if comparisons were made at the community level. Moreover, available data severely qualify the conventional assumption that unemployment in Mexico is directly associated with emigration—the vast majority of emigrants had jobs in Mexico prior to leaving for the United States.

The point here is not to contradict the notions that migrant families suffer economic deprivation in Mexico and that their principal motivation for leaving is to find employment. There is also little doubt that a further deterioration of Mexico's economy, given circumstances prevalent in 1987, will provide additional incentives for emigration. But it is worth underscoring that the problem is not "simply" one of creating more jobs: Many of the communities and households that send migrants to the United States have counterparts, identically situated in socioeconomic terms, that do not send any migrants at all. Moreover, the migration that has occurred in the past has not been principally the result of Mexican Government action or inaction; the direct impact of government policies on emigration has not been as large as popular conceptions suggest.

Ironically, in Mexican politics, too, it is frequently perceptions, rather than complex conclusions based on research, that matter. The perception in Mexico that emigration is proof of domestic economic inadequacies is decades old, and it is likely to be strengthened by the current economic crisis. In Mexico, there are now no groups demanding that the government prevent the departure of undocumented migrants; however, in the future, potentially innumerable groups could demand that the government create additional jobs in order to make it unnecessary for Mexicans to leave their country to work in the United States.

The politics of emigration are thus complex and sensitive. These domestic sensitivities are, by themselves, probably insurmountable obstacles to Mexico's engaging the United States in substantive bilateral negotiations regarding migration control.

Migration Control: Divergent U.S. and Mexican Objectives

Domestic politics in the United States and Mexico seem to generate a negative response to the question of whether a bilateral approach is desirable in achieving migration control. The response is explicit in the case of the United States, and implicit in that of Mexico. The predominant U.S. attitude is that there is no point in bothering with such an approach as long as an acceptable unilateral approach is available; the predominant Mexican attitude, as illustrated by past avoidance of initiative in this area, is that *no* other approach is likely to improve upon the status quo.

Domestic political constraints, however, are only part of the explanation for this impasse. Another important reason involves the largely incompatible objectives of the two governments regarding their perceptions of migration control and the policy instruments they are willing to use to achieve it. These objectives have not been publicly articulated in quite the same terms as those expressed below, but it is clear that the immediate concerns of the two governments are fundamentally different, if not entirely at odds.

The U.S. political and legislative objective expressed countless times during the process that led to IRCA was to reduce undocumented migration in the short term. This objective has been of little interest to Mexico, principally because the short-term focus would require Mexico to cooperate by using force to restrain emigration from its territory. Legally, such action would probably violate Mexico's Constitution; morally, it would be a violation of basic human rights; politically, it could be very costly. To accede to a U.S. request for this type of cooperation makes no sense to Mexico. Such action, in fact, is unthinkable, and the only reason the topic has even been addressed explicitly is that it has been suggested repeatedly, though informally, by U.S. Government officials. When considering why these requests are so unattractive, Mexicans are sometimes reminded of the negative experiences they endured in the mid-1950s, when their government attempted similar control measures as a natural result of its participation in the *bracero* program.

In Mexico, emigration control, as such, is rarely expressed as an important concern. Given the definition of migration control employed in this paper, however, it is possible to suggest that the preeminent short-term Mexican objective regarding such control is to obtain the regularization of the legal status of undocumented Mexicans. But this objective is not popular in the United States, as the resistance of many key groups and of public opinion to the inclusion of legalization in the immigration reform legislation illustrates. More importantly, at least for the time being, the issue is moot. IRCA has already provided for the legalization of several hundred thousand Mexicans, and the possibility of persuading the United States to promote legislation to legalize those remaining is small.

The long-term Mexican objective most often articulated is to utilize development and employment-generation schemes to reduce the incentives for emigration. However, domestic resources for such projects are, for all practical purposes, nonexistent. Furthermore, although the new law established a commission to study multilateral economic cooperation with countries of origin, judging from the immigration debate itself and, more broadly, from the limited role that the United States has thus far envisioned for itself in assisting Mexican economic recovery in recent years, it seems clear that these Mexican long-term interests are not shared by the U.S. Government.

To the extent that the United States has not been able to restrain undocumented Mexican immigration through unilateral measures, its principal interest in a bilateral approach is in having Mexico restrain nationals as they leave for the United States. The enactment of the new U.S. law does not alter this emphasis, although it could reduce some of the pressure within the United States for further control measures. Mexican initiatives regarding emigration control seem unlikely. Bringing the issue to public attention would probably generate criticism of Mexican Government shortcomings that would not be easy to address. And resolving the matter at the negotiating table would entail deflecting U.S. requests for police action and persuading U.S. representatives that alternative long-term strategies, although not attractive north of the border, should be considered. Given these circumstances, the Mexican side of the migration control problem remains at a stalemate.

The Future

The Immigration Reform and Control Act of 1986 is the most ambitious action the United States has taken to reduce undocumented migration since Operation Wetback, a mass deportation campaign conducted in mid-1954. From Mexico's perspective, it is probably the most important challenge in the area of binational migration issues since the termination of the *bracero* program in 1964. Even though the net effects of the legislation are not likely to close the "safety valve" as abruptly or as tightly as commonly thought, slowing down emigration could have adverse effects in some regions of Mexico, at a time of economic and political uncertainty. If Mexico's general economic situation deteriorates, as is quite possible, the United States, too, could become sensitive to the negative consequences of its immigration policy in Mexico.

Given that Mexico's economic difficulties are likely to continue for some time and that U.S. immigration policy is perceived to add to this burden, one of the governments, or perhaps both, will likely feel a need to continue bilateral discussions on migration issues. It would not be unreasonable to expect more formal, though perhaps modest, bilateral exchanges, to keep options open in the event that the worst-case scenarios of IRCA materialize or, at least, to demonstrate goodwill. As previously mentioned, the new U.S. law itself mandates consultations with Mexico, and as U.S. immigration policies reverberate south of the border, these meetings are likely to constitute the minimum U.S.–Mexican dialogue that will occur during the next few years.

The new law not only seeks to reduce undocumented immigration; it also attempts to partially make up for that reduction. It does this by legalizing some migrants, facilitating the admission of temporary workers for agricultural employment under the H-2A and SAW (Special Agricultural Worker) provisions, and establishing a mechanism, to go into effect in the 1990s, that provides for the legalization or recruitment of additional agricultural workers if the U.S. executive branch determines that a labor shortage exists.

Some commentators have interpreted the agricultural labor provisions of the law as providing the basis for the bilateral management of agricultural worker flows into the United States. Though such arrangements could in fact occur, the United States is not likely to require active Mexican cooperation in the implementation of these aspects of the law. Nor is it clear that the current U.S. administration would seek to engage Mexico in a formal role or, if it did, what that role would be. Certainly, IRCA does not envision a labor recruitment role for Mexico, or any other foreign country, in any way similar to that provided for in the post-World War II *bracero* agreements. Legalization is expected to occur according to conditions of individual eligibility and, therefore, does not constitute a recruitment mechanism. In the case of the H-2A sections of the statute, it is the employer who has the preeminent role of determining for which workers to solicit temporary visas. And if the United States proposed a labor recruitment role for Mexico in the manner of the *bracero* program, it is not clear that Mexico could accept the role in the 1980s and 1990s and still avoid the responsibility of using force to prevent illegal entries into the United States.

Those who have argued, in Mexico and in the United States, that the bilateral management of U.S.–Mexican migration is desirable in itself have ignored the existence of fundamental differences in national objectives. Whatever the bilateral management of migration is, it is a means to an end, and not an end in itself. The record of U.S.–Mexican dialogue suggests that whatever the national ends with respect to migration have been perceived to be, a bilateral approach to them has been considered either undesirable or unfeasible. We hope that if genuine opportunities for other kinds of cooperation do arise, they are not missed, and that the unbridgeable gaps that do exist are not viewed as minor problems whose solutions require merely sufficient goodwill and a bilateral approach.

The New Immigration Law and Mexico

Doris M. Meissner

There is no consensus in Mexico or the United States on the new Simpson-Rodino immigration legislation and its consequences. Mexico and the United States need to create a bilateral institution to exchange information on a continuous basis regarding implementation and the implications of the legislation. The implementation issues fall into three main categories: 1) legalization, 2) strengthened enforcement and 3) research and future policy. Such structured information exchange could generate greater trust and respect between Mexico and the United States, and perhaps contribute to the resolution of other problems between the two countries.

O N NOVEMBER 6, 1986, President Reagan signed into law immigration control measures that had been under active consideration for at least five years by the Congress and publicly debated for more than a decade. Hailed as a landmark reform, the Immigration Reform and Control Act (IRCA) was intended to enable the United States to "regain control of our borders," the phrase that became a byword for those concerned about growing illegal immigration in the United States.

Changes in U.S. immigration law and practice are of critical importance to Mexico, the major single source of illegal migration to the United States. Mexico's initial reaction to the new U.S. immigration law was measured. The lower house of Mexico's Congress passed a resolution expressing "regret" over the action, calling the law "discriminatory in spirit" and "detrimental" to Mexico's interests. But the government did not make the bill's passage a public issue. In December, 1986, President de la Madrid told the official newspaper, *El Nacional*, that he thought "the greatest effect of the new law will not be caused by massive deportations of workers to Mexico, at least at levels significantly higher than the present." What officials did predict was a significant decrease in the number of people attempting to migrate to the United States in the belief that American employers would no

92

longer hire illegal alien workers. Mr. de la Madrid acknowledged the importance of this potential change by observing that "any reduction in the flow of migration toward the United States can be a serious element in the development of Mexico, since this factor has served as a mechanism of adjustment in regard to employment."

For a nation that has been unable to create up to one million jobs a year needed for new entrants to the labor force, the migration safety valve has eased the impact of widespread underemployment and unemployment. Migration north has been an integral part of Mexico's economy, political assumptions, and social structure for decades. Thus, the shift in U.S. policy, although taken for domestic policy reasons, has palpable foreign policy consequences.

Public statements by Mexican officials decrying the law have become increasingly strident. Media coverage has been extensive and highly charged. The Mexican press warns of mass deportations calling the new law "strongly anti-Mexican," and based on "discrimination and persecution of people with coffee-colored skin." Similar assessments come from government officials, labor leaders and even members of the church hierarchy. Acknowledging that the United States has the sovereign right and need to assert control over foreign entries, there is a strongly expressed fear that the law is harmful to Mexico. This has bred deepening resentment and the growing feeling that IRCA is tantamount to an unfriendly foreign policy declaration against Mexico by its powerful northern neighbor.

In a clear shift from its traditional stance, Mexico has begun to take a more active role on migration matters in the United States. In concert with the consulates of El Salvador, Colombia, Honduras and Guatemala, Mexico has joined with local attorneys and social agencies in Houston to file a lawsuit to "safeguard the rights and privileges" of illegal immigrants. The successful verdict sent a nationwide warning to employers who might fire aliens that can qualify for legalization. Despite the policy of nonintervention that has been a linchpin of Mexico's foreign policy, Mexico is participating in the Houston task force project to publish a "black list" of unscrupulous immigration consultants and attorneys known to give immigrants inaccurate information or charge excessively high fees.

In another shift, Mexican–American regional leaders have been invited to Mexico to discuss immigration issues with government officials, including President de la Madrid. Such exchanges have occurred in the past but there seems to be new energy in them. Mexican–Americans who have been involved speculate that the immigration issue may create conditions for Mexico to advance a more politicized agenda with the United States.

There is, however, a contradictory theme that is also pervasive.

"The law is going to be obeyed, but is not going to be complied with . . . Mexicans are going to continue crossing the border," said the chairman of the Mexican Chamber of Deputies' Border Affairs Committee. The governor of the state of Zacatecas, a source of sizeable flows, has flatly declared that the law will not work. Mexicans have crossed the border to find work, he says, because thousands of U.S. businesses have welcomed their labor and will continue to do so.

Another politician in that state is philosophical in a different way. "It will hurt us for a year or two, but it's going to be a very expensive law for the United States. Then you will once again want our laborers, and the law will be changed or forgotten."

So there is no clear consensus in Mexico about the change or its consequences just as there is divided opinion in the United States over these issues. The legalization provisions, the first parts of the bill to be implemented, are likely to be quite generous to Mexicans. The enforcement provisions, which will not be fully implemented until June 1988, are likely to constrict the illegal flow of Mexicans to the United States over the longer term.

From the standpoint of our bilateral relations, migration deserves sustained attention in our diplomacy, with law enforcement no longer the core framework for discussion. Congress pointed the way by instructing the executive branch to consult with Mexico on implementation of the law. The Commissioner of the U.S. Immigration and Naturalization Service (INS) has travelled to Mexico City twice since the law passed. He met with all the relevant senior government officials, including the President, and with the press. The U.S. message has been that the law is a legitimate, modest measure to regulate migration and foster assimilation of immigrants, and is not unlike that of other nations, including Mexico. Furthermore, in pursuing the law's central provision—penalties against employers who hire illegal migrants—large-scale deportation efforts will not be made.

But the essential step has not been taken. The two countries should form a bilateral body for ongoing information exchange on the implementation and implications of the legislation.

Issues that create irritants are arising regularly. One Mexican senator has condemned the U. S. decision to "deport more than two million Mexicans." The Mexican press has reported that the border has been heavily reinforced with new agents to stop Mexican crossers. Both assertions are incorrect. They provide examples of the seeds of serious misunderstandings that can be averted if we provide for accurate, timely information exchange. The change in U.S. policy could heighten tension in the relationship, or it could serve as an opportunity to look anew at the migration problem with the objective of managing it as rationally as possible.

There are literally hundreds of implementation issues of potential interest for U.S.–Mexican relations. They fall into three broad areas: legalization; strengthened enforcement; and research and future policy. The following items could constitute an agenda of bilateral issues for consideration, as both nations prepare to elect new presidents.

I. Legalization Measures

IRCA provides two forms of legalization (amnesty) for persons illegally in the United States. General legalization applies to persons who can demonstrate "continuous unlawful residence" in the United States since at least January 1, 1982. The second, known as the special agricultural worker provisions (SAW), authorizes legal status for persons who can demonstrate that they worked in agriculture for at least 90 days between May 1, 1985, and May 1, 1986.

A. Legalization

Legalization was a highly controversial measure and secured passage by only a few votes. The January 1, 1982, eligibility date for the general legalization was arbitrarily chosen by Congress. It reflects a political judgment rather than an analysis of the proportion or groups among the illegal alien population that should be granted legal status. As a result, half or more of the illegal alien population in the United States may be ineligible to apply. The law is silent regarding this group. Theoretically, these people will return to their home countries as employer sanctions take effect and work becomes increasingly difficult to find. In fact, these people are likely to remain and be driven further into the underground economy.

Thus, this group is and perceives itself to be very vulnerable. Fears that the United States might precipitously "dump" potentially hundreds of thousands of people across the border are always close to the surface. The Immigration and Naturalization Service (INS) has regularly made statements that it has neither the resources nor the inclination to mount special efforts to locate and remove aliens not eligible for legalization. This policy must be regularly restated and communicated to Mexico.

The application period for eligible persons to file for legalization began May 5, 1987, and is authorized to run for one year. Successful applicants obtain temporary resident status for a period of 18 months, after which time they are eligible to apply for permanent resident ("green card") status. Five years after receiving green cards, they may apply for citizenship. Although estimates are inherently imprecise, more than 1 million Mexican nationals are likely to apply for this program.

At the midway point of the legalization program, 758,387 applications had been filed. Almost 70 percent are Mexican, a significantly higher proportion than the 40 to 50 percent of the illegal population believed to be from Mexico. This has been a surprise that belies the widely held view that Mexican migrants live in Mexico and work part of the year in the United States, making the migration a temporary movement of people between the two countries. Instead, there is a sizeable group that has been in the United States continuously for at least five years and intends to remain.

Although the legalization is working more strongly to the benefit of Mexicans than other nationality groups, the overall application level has been somewhat disappointing. About 97 percent of the applications filed are being approved. The statutory prohibition against the use of information offered through the legalization process for enforcement purposes is being observed. A surge of applications will presumably occur during the final months of the program in spring 1988. Congress could also vote to extend the legalization period. However, in light of the narrow margin by which the program was enacted, this is unlikely even though a vigorous debate on that question will probably take place.

There are several key issues that provide additional insight into the actual workings of the program. Policy in these areas has been articulated in public statements or through published, written regulations.

1. Eligibility and Evidence Requirements. For most eligible persons, amassing evidence to prove eligibility is difficult. Surviving undetected in the United States has meant living without the familiar panoply of bank, credit, and personal accounting records that most of us employ to verify residence. Although the majority of illegal aliens are paid by employers in accordance with legal requirements, a substantial portion have either been paid under the table or have not retained payment records. Employer affidavits are excellent corroboration of residence, but some employers are reluctant to provide them if they skirted tax filing requirements. The Internal Revenue Service (IRS) has announced that it will not make special efforts to locate employers of illegal aliens for tax liability. However, it says, it also will not overlook cases that come to its attention. For possibly guilty parties, this is not strong reassurance. INS, however, has affirmed that it will not pass on to the IRS information submitted by employers to corroborate individual legalization claims.

The government is allowing applicants to present documents—principally social security records or numbers, or driver's licenses—that prove residence in accordance with the requirements of the legalization program, but that are fraudulent in that they belong to fictitious persons or to persons other than the applicant and were obtained to conceal the alien's identity.

It is not allowing witnesses to appear and make sworn statements regarding residence in the United States on behalf of an alien who has incomplete documentation or none at all. This is unfortunate, for there are precedents for such allowances in the experiences of other nations. France, in a 1981 legalization program, for example, allowed affidavits; about 15 percent of the applicants exercised that option. Thus, the provision did not open up an avenue for abuse, but provided a way to address the unique circumstances in which illegals find themselves. It also demonstrated good faith by the government, an intangible but critical element for program success.

After some early tension between the INS and assistance agencies, a reasonable understanding has developed with regard to evidence. INS has been open to a wide variety of types of proof including divorce decrees and children's report cards, for example. In addition, the state of California, where more than half of the applications have been filed, is providing education and tax records to assist applicants. And Mexico's Foreign Minister, Bernardo Sepulveda, announced that consulates in the United States had been directed to help Mexican nationals obtain birth certificates, passports and other identification documents needed by U.S. authorities.

2. Family Members of Legalized Persons. The prevailing migration pattern has been for one family member to come to the United States, establish work and living arrangements and be joined by family members here later. Thus, there are many cases where all members of the family unit may not be eligible. ("Family" in immigration language means spouse, children, and, in the case of minors, parents.) Of all the issues in the legalization program, this one remains the most contentious.

Where all family members are not eligible, those who are have been wary about applying, for fear of revealing the deportability of their relatives. INS failed to clarify its policy in such cases until five months into the program when it announced that minor children who are ineligible will be granted humanitarian relief only if both parents are eligible; ineligible spouses may obtain it only under exceptional circumstances but not if the "only claim to . . . relief is by virtue of the marriage itself."

The problem stems from the Congress' unwillingness, in writing the law, to allow ineligible family members to qualify on the basis of family relationship. This presents a contradiction with the principle of family unity, the traditional underpinning of the U.S. immigration system. However, the Attorney General could exercise his discretionary authority to stay the deportation of persons in the United States in favor of family members of amnesty recipients for humanitarian reasons.

In reality, immediate relatives are probably not at much actual risk. INS will not move to deport them, due to a lack of sufficient resources, unless they are discovered in employment checks. But split-eligibility families believe they are at risk and some significant proportion may not apply for legalization as a result.

In cases where family members are outside the United States, newly legalized persons will be able to petition, after eighteen months, for their immigration. Especially for Mexico, where the current waiting period is almost ten years, this will increase demand on an already over-subscribed legal immigration system. This additional pressure on the immigration system is likely to lead Congress to revise current laws. Mexicans, along with nationals of several other countries—Korea, the Philippines, and Cuba, for example—will be the principal beneficiaries of such modifications, should they occur.

3. Continuous Residence. A key phrase in the law is the requirement that persons show "continuous lawful residence" in the United States since at least January 1, 1982. The statute goes on, however, to state that "brief, casual, and innocent absences" will be allowed. The interpretation of "brief, casual, and innocent" is important for Mexican applicants.

Continuous residence is not considered to have been broken if the applicant's absences from the United States are less than 45 days in any one year or a total of 180 days since January 1, 1982. Decisions within this guideline are made with a case-by-case review of factors such as the purposes for travel to Mexico, children's school location, and location of major assets—home, automobile, or insurance policies, for example. This is a generous standard and incorporates the reality of migration patterns, particularly those from Mexico.

Except for the family unity question, then, policies and procedures for administering the legalization are proving to be reasonable. INS has been willing to reconsider early decisions and has made some adjustments in its policies. Observers remain hopeful that this attitude will continue to prevail so that additional adjustments are made before the end of the program to encourage the maximum possible participation by eligible aliens of all nations.

B. Special Agricultural Worker Program

Of all the provisions of the legislation, the SAW program is the least understood and most unpredictable. It was designed in haste and amended to the bill as a political necessity to garner needed votes from members of Congress representing agribusiness constituencies. It discriminates in favor of one class of illegal aliens, persons who can show they worked in agriculture at least 90 days during the year ending May 1, 1986. Such persons receive virtually the same benefits as aliens qualified for the general legalization. Although generous toward one class of illegal aliens, its purpose was to assure stability in the foreign labor supply for one category of employer, growers of perishable crops.

The application period is different from and longer than that for legalization. It began June 1, 1987, and runs for eighteen months, concluding on December 1, 1989. The beneficiaries of the program are almost exclusively Mexican nationals. Estimates are that only about 15 percent of Mexican nationals who migrate to the United States work in agriculture. Nevertheless, about 350,000 persons may qualify for the program.

Only growers of "perishable commodities" can qualify to employ SAW workers. Defining such crops has been an intensely political process wherein Christmas trees, for example, are included but sugar cane is not. Southwest agriculture, where Mexican workers are virtually the single group affected, has been generously treated in the program; it potentially benefits Mexico and Mexican workers significantly.

Still, agricultural employers have been extremely vocal about the inevitability of crop failures due to labor shortages. In fact, in the major harvests since IRCA passed, shortages never materialized and several new records—strawberries and apples, for example, in the Northwest—have been set.

Controversy over agricultural worker issues will continue because the law allows for "replenishment workers" beginning in 1991, if agricultural labor needs can be demonstrated. These workers, if authorized, would have the same opportunity for permanent status in the United States as those eligible for the SAW program.

Thus, the SAW program establishes special immigration provisions that could substantially augment legal Mexican migration to the United States through the agricultural sector for the foreseeable future. This has ramifications for both countries that merit careful exploration and analysis.

II. Strengthened Enforcement

Employer sanctions and increased border enforcement are sensitive issues for U.S.–Mexican relations. Even if they interrupt the flow only partially or slow its rate of growth, the impact on Mexico could be substantial.

A. Employer Sanctions

The centerpiece of the legislation and the impetus for its passage was employer sanctions. The American public accepts the idea that if businesses can no longer employ illegal aliens with impunity, migration flows will be diminished.

Sanctions became effective December 1, 1986, with an employer education effort during the first six months. For the 12 months beginning June 1, 1987, only warnings are issued to first-time violators. The law then goes fully into effect after this 18-month preparation period. At that time, it will apply to newly hired persons, not to those already employed. Employers must request evidence of citizenship or permanent residence as part of the hiring process for all job applicants— natives and foreigners, citizens and noncitizens, alike. Employers are not responsible for assessing the validity of identification documents. They must make the inquiry, obtain the applicant's statement that the documents are valid, and be able to demonstrate that they have done so. The law also provides for a special counsel to be established in the Department of Justice to handle complaints of employer discrimination based on alienage. This is a new concept in U.S. law, which was developed to counteract the potential for hiring discrimination against foreigners that could result from employer sanctions.

Because it is impossible for the government to enforce such a law through actual checks of all employers, the effectiveness of sanctions rests on voluntary compliance. Historically, voluntary compliance has proved to be an effective method for achieving similar broad social policy goals in areas such as taxation, minimum wage laws, and child labor restrictions. The success of employer sanctions will depend on the government's ability to educate employers, target frequent violators, engage in random compliance reviews, and, ultimately, undertake successful prosecutions.

Congress has appropriated adequate resources for the first year of sanctions but the real test is reductions in employment of aliens not authorized to work and in illegal immigration flows. One year after enactment of IRCA, there has been a 30 percent decline in border apprehensions. This is an encouraging sign, but it is too new to be pronounced a trend.

Whichever party controls the White House and Congress in the future, the commitment to employer enforcement must be systematic and continuing. A worst-case scenario would be wide fluctuations in levels of expenditure or effort as a function of politics or the state of the economy. Should this occur, Mexico would realize its deepest concern about the new law: immigration enforcement as a tool to manipulate Mexico.

Issues that should be of particular interest for U.S.–Mexican relations include the level and distribution of resources directed at sanctions enforcement; the geographic areas and labor-market sectors selected for enforcement; the type and disposition of alienage discrimination complaints; the degree of compliance; the changes in hiring and working conditions resulting from sanctions; and the effect of sanctions on illegal alien flows and behavior.

B. Strengthened Border Enforcement

The companion to sanctions in Congress' scheme is strengthened border enforcement, optimum enforcement consisting of preventing illegal entry altogether.

The U.S.–Mexico border separates two nations with wider income disparities than any other contiguous countries in the world. Border issues have become increasingly sensitive from both a management and a political standpoint. As border enforcement increases, the challenge of checking illegal activity while minimizing onerous restraints on the legal movement of goods and people will become increasingly important to the economic well-being of both countries.

U.S. Border Patrol resources were augmented by the largest single increment in history during fiscal year 1986. The new law authorizes a 50 percent increase in that enlarged base. This additional resource expansion, currently underway, consists of both personnel and technology. The technology includes computerized sensor systems that pinpoint illegal crossings, thereby helping officers to make arrests;

high-vision scopes, through which officers can "see" people at night; low-light television that spans urban and heavily populated crossing areas; helicopters with searchlights; and mobile radio and communication equipment.

Key Mexican policy-makers and staff should visit the border and observe operations at close range. Issues of particular interest include the proportion of Mexican and non-Mexican nationals among illegal border crossers; the level and distribution of new resources; data regarding the number of people actually crossing, rather than the number of apprehensions made at the border; changes in the flow of illegal immigrants during the post-legalization period of employer sanctions; and the impact of the SAW provisions on border operations.

III. Research and Future Policy

For both nations, policymaking on illegal migration has been severely hampered by a dearth of information. This is partly endemic, and partly due to inattention. The new law provides landmark opportunities for increased knowledge of issues that are central to future planning and policymaking. Both countries have relied on often incomplete or specious data to support analysis that reinforces respective political positions.

Research should be directed at analyzing the changes in migration flows and nationalities; states of origin; destination; age; sex; family composition; education; employment history; income; type of work; labor-market mobility; remittances; number of relatives within and outside the United States; participation in social services, education, and health care systems; apprehension history; and reasons for migrating.

One vehicle for such research is the two study commissions mandated by IRCA. One is to study agricultural labor needs of the United States; the other is to analyze international migration and economic development. Each is authorized for three years. Skeptics see commissions as window dressing, but that characterization may not be accurate in this case. The genesis of the new law can be traced to the findings and recommendations of another congressionally mandated commission, the Select Commission on Immigration and Refugee Policy. The new commissions will function as the next generation of that exercise. They can be expected to play a pivotal role in shaping public attitudes and future policy toward migration in the United States.

Mexico chose not to play a role in the work of the Select Commission. It can and should play a role in the coming cycle.

IV. Conclusion

The new immigration law sets the stage for a serious, new binational experiment. It is by no means clear what the effects will be for either nation. Migration pressures spring from economic stagnation, population dynamics, demand for low-wage labor, and daunting income differentials between the two countries. Structured information exchange will not alter those forces. But it can create a forum for discussion regarding events and problems that can lead to serious misunderstandings if channels of communication are not carefully cultivated. The implicit hope is that through improved communications, even in an area of strong disagreement such as migration has been, greater trust and respect will develop and create one more pathway for progress on the larger, long-range problems that the United States and Mexico share.

Part IV
U.S.–Mexico Relations

On the Formulation of a U.S. Policy Toward Mexico

José Juan de Olloqui

The United States has generally ignored Mexico, except when issues of national security are involved. A well-defined U.S. policy, based on mutual respect and the recognition that the two countries have different interests, is sorely needed. In formulating such a comprehensive policy, the United States should realize that noninterference in Mexico's internal politics serves U.S. security interests. For the same reason, the U.S. should also work to strengthen Mexico's economy by reducing U.S. protectionism, encouraging the flow of U.S. capital to Mexico and helping resolve the debt crisis. Bilateral conflict over the drug issue could be reduced if the United States dealt with the problem on its side of the border. Finally, the United States should respect the rule of law in seeking solutions to regional conflicts and not regard Mexico's independent foreign policy as aggression directed against the United States.

A S OF TODAY, THE United States has still not elaborated a coherent policy toward Mexico. This situation, commonly known as "benign neglect," should instead be called "malign neglect," because of its detrimental effects. The U.S. Government has allowed its Mexican policy to be guided strictly by circumstantial interests and criteria, acting only when faced with specific problems.

There is, however, one aspect of U.S.–Mexican relations that seems to receive constant U.S. attention: the safeguarding of national security. However, the concept of what Mexico implies for the United States has changed from one administration to another; even within a single administration, there has been no agreement on this issue among the various government agencies.

These circumstances lead one to believe that Mexico is not, and never has been, a priority of U.S. foreign policy. Perhaps this is because the United States regards Mexico as simply another developing nation, with all the weaknesses and defects that are associated with these countries. However, this view does not take into account a set of peculiarities that distinguish Mexico from other developing countries.

The United States should be aware that its fate is strongly linked to that of Mexico. Because of their geographic proximity, neither country can choose to ignore its neighbor. This fact alone should lead the U.S. Government to formulate a well-defined policy toward Mexico.

But geographic proximity is not the only reason to devise such a policy. Mexico is the third largest trading partner of the United States; it is the most important oil supplier to its northern neighbor; its people comprise the largest national group of tourists in the United States; and 35 percent of its foreign debt is with U.S. banks. Consequently, fluctuations in the Mexican economy can provoke serious repercussions in the United States. For example, according to present banking regulations, if Mexico were not able to pay its debt, or should it decide not to do so, many creditor banks would be faced with a difficult financial situation; some would even be forced to declare bankruptcy. The result would be chaos in the U.S. financial system.

Aside from these physical, demographic, and economic reasons, another important aspect makes Mexico uniquely important to the United States: Approximately 15 million U.S. citizens are of Mexican descent and still maintain close cultural, economic, and family ties with their native country. This means that there is significant participation of Mexican–Americans in internal U.S. politics, especially in certain states that are electorally important, such as Texas and California.

Finally, Mexico's specific importance to the United States must be considered in terms of U.S. national security. Mexico is a significant provider of raw materials to the United States. It also shares a 2000 mile border with its northern neighbor that is basically unprotected. In spite of the border's length and permeability, however, it does not represent a direct military threat to the United States, because Mexico would never attempt an attack. It is also improbable that Mexico would allow itself to be used as a conduit by a nation attempting military aggression against the United States (in a situation reminiscent of the "Zimmerman telegram" incident)[1], just as Mexico would not allow the United States to use Mexican territory to attack any other country.

Since national security is the principal and constant interest of the United States, it is hypersensitive and unwilling to make concessions on this issue. As a result, it is concerned with the security threat represented by the potential penetration of ideologies contrary to its own into Mexico and its neighboring countries. In principle, the U.S. Government supports social change and democratization, but when a choice has to be made between these principles and what it considers its national security interests, the United States will not hesitate to decide in favor of the latter.

Precisely because of the unique ties between Mexico and the United States, the lack of a well-defined and comprehensive U.S. foreign policy regarding Mexico is remarkable. Even more surprising is the fact that the United States rarely takes into consideration the Mexican point of view when deciding on matters of common interest within a bilateral, regional, or multilateral context. The U.S. Government has systematically ignored Mexico's opinions and insisted on treating Mexico as a pawn, which can be moved without consultation, according to interests that are not always shared. On more than one occasion, this has put Mexico in a difficult and unwarranted position, resulting in a deterioration of the bilateral relationship because of open and public disagreement.

Thus, the lack of a specific U.S. policy toward Mexico has complicated the relationship between the two countries and contributed to creating unnecessary tensions in a relationship that, by its very nature, has always been difficult.

Basis for an Agreement

In order to improve the relationship between the two countries and to normalize the policy that is to regulate it, the United States must be aware that as a rich and powerful country, it has interests that will not always coincide with those of a developing nation such as Mexico; moreover, the respective interests of the two may frequently be in opposition. The United States must come to terms with the fact that Mexico will place its own interests above everything else.

Therefore, better understanding and greater cooperation between these countries will be possible only if they are based on an attitude of mutual respect, without any external pressures. Additionally, when these pressures become public, they generate great resentment among Mexicans, thereby limiting the possibilities of negotiation and of the smooth operation of bilateral relations.

In elaborating a global policy toward Mexico, the U.S. Government should learn to take Mexico's point of view into consideration; Mexico is among the top 15 countries in the world by any indicator (except military), has considerable influence in an international context, and has frequently acted as a spokesman, and even as a leader, for other countries with similar problems. Just as the United States consults with its industrialized allies concerning certain matters, it should consult with Mexico on others. If this argument is valid with regard to regional conflicts, it is much more so concerning bilateral problems. The recent case of the Simpson–Rodino immigration bill serves as an explicit example. Even if, strictly speaking, U.S. immigration law is an internal matter of the United States, its effect on Mexico is significant enough to warrant a bilateral agreement on the subject.

Traditionally, there have been three areas of conflict between Mexico and the United States: boundaries and waters, undocumented workers, and trade. Other areas of contention have surfaced more recently: oil, drug trafficking, foreign debt, and differing views concerning certain international conflicts, especially in Central America and the Caribbean.

On the basis of mutual respect and a recognition of the differences between the two countries, the United States can begin to build a clear and coherent policy toward Mexico that will deal with all of these matters. The following suggestions could serve as a guide in designing a comprehensive policy.

Security

The U.S. Government's major security concerns are a politically unstable Mexico or the coming to power of a Mexican regime that is hostile to the United States. These fears have produced some interference in Mexican affairs, most recently in the form of support from some groups in the United States to an opposing political party in Mexico. This action was apparently based on the notion that Mexico should have a two-party system similar to that of the United States, instead of allowing Mexican democracy to develop according to the characteristics of its own society. This kind of interference is not only unacceptable but dangerous: Because it contributes to the destabilization of Mexico, it is contrary to U.S. interests and, perhaps, to those of a large part of the Latin American subcontinent. U.S. interference with the Mexican political system through this type of action could throw the delicate political balance toward the left, instead of the right, as some people in the United States expect. Americans should keep in mind that Mexico has a long revolutionary tradition.

Even if the views of the Mexican Government are different from, and sometimes conflict with, those of the United States, they do not necessarily pose a challenge or a threat to U.S. national security, because in spite of their differences, the two countries have many common interests, among them the maintenance of regional stability. The Mexican Government has a splendid record in this regard, with a history of over 60 years of peaceful government. During this period, with only one exception, Mexican presidents have concluded their terms in office, and the deceased former presidents have died of natural causes. Not many countries in the region can claim a similar stability.

The Mexican political system is a result of the Mexican Revolution, which occurred seven years prior to the Russian Revolution and almost 50 years before the Cuban one. Mexico has no interest in exporting its revolution, and it does not import others. However, Mexico is both firm and categorical in its demand for respect for pluralism of ideologies, especially in Latin America.

Economic Relations

One of the main objectives in elaborating a policy with regard to Mexico is to attain a balanced and mutually beneficial economic relationship.

The economic asymmetry between the two countries is undeniable; therefore, any new policy should contribute to correcting this asymmetry or, at least, to decreasing it. Strengthening the Mexican economy would help to stabilize the country; it would also allow Mexico to obtain the funds it requires to cope with its foreign financial obligations, and would help to reduce the flow of undocumented workers to the United States.

To facilitate the development of mutually beneficial bilateral economic relations, the United States should consider the following suggestions:

1. Reduce or eliminate the protectionist measures that obstruct Mexican exports to the U.S. market. It would be useful to establish a plan to assure an annual minimum level of foreign currency for Mexico, which would enable Mexico to plan for its economic growth. This level could be guaranteed by a U.S. commitment to purchase a fixed dollar amount of products.
2. Encourage the flow of U.S. capital toward Mexico through direct investment or financial credits. A mechanism that would help to increase the amount of funds available for foreign investment, and would benefit both countries, is the conversion of debt into equity, which is now being experimented with on a small scale. This would enable Mexico to reduce its foreign debt and increase foreign investment, while permitting American investors to participate in Mexican enterprises within Mexico's legal framework.
3. Establish an interdepartmental committee in the U.S. Government to watch over U.S.–Mexican relations and to coordinate the pertinent policies and administrative measures of the various government agencies. The Carter administration implemented a

similar project, but the coordinating apparatus lacked the requisite executive clout. Therefore, the proposed committee would have to have the necessary political backing in order to be effective and play more than a nominal, coordinating role. Problems originating in the decentralized structure of the American political system would thus be solved. This committee should be an ad hoc group designed to solve urgent and concrete problems.

In summary, I suggest the formulation of an economic policy that would allow Mexico, through the export of its goods and services, as well as through an increase in coinvestments and the flow of capital, to reactivate its economy and thereby generate the funds it needs to deal with its financial obligations. President Miguel de la Madrid has recently said: "The dead do not pay, and those who are broke cannot be clients." I would add: If Mexico cannot export its products, it will probably end up exporting its men.

Undocumented Workers

The problem of migrating workers cannot be solved through legislation; this phenomenon is caused by many socioeconomic factors, which have been aggravated by Mexico's economic crisis. There is an urgency to create enough jobs in Mexico. Even though Mexico has reduced its rate of demographic growth from 3.5 percent to 1.9 percent over the past fifteen years, it must still provide almost one million jobs a year simply to satisfy the increase in its labor force.

But lack of jobs in Mexico is not the only reason that Mexican workers emigrate to the United States. The difference in the level of development of the two countries and the opportunities available to immigrant workers in the United States also contribute to the perpetuation of this phenomenon.

For the United States, undocumented workers are not just a burden; on the contrary, they represent a positive element in the economy. In fact, were it not for illegal workers, many marginal lands would never be cultivated, and much hard labor would never be accomplished; above all, many enterprises would not make the same profits if they had to hire more expensive labor.

Undocumented workers fulfill a necessary and useful role by providing a cheap source of labor that helps to make production more competitive. This argument should not be minimized, especially considering that the U.S. trade deficit originated not in a lack of capital, technology, or managerial skills, but in the high cost of labor. Moreover, it has been proved that immigrant workers pay their taxes and do not make use of many government services; therefore, their net contribution to the economy is positive.

If the United States sincerely wishes to discourage the flow of Mexican workers into its territory, in spite of the advantages they represent, the best way to do so is to help reactivate Mexico's economy. Building a Berlin Wall (as has sometimes been suggested) or categorically refusing to admit Mexicans into the United States would be an offense not only to Mexico, but to all of Latin America. On the other hand, the United States cannot expect the Mexican Government to prevent its citizens from leaving the country; this would violate the Mexican Constitution and is a practice that the United States itself has always disapproved of when carried out by other countries.

I offer the following practical suggestions for handling this problem:

1. Encourage direct investment in the regions from which most immigrant workers come. With a substantial contribution of capital (for example, in agro-industry), emigration from these areas would greatly diminish.

2. Negotiate an agreement between Mexico and the United States that establishes the number of legal workers allowed to cross the border, the places where they may work, their labor rights, and the terms of their eventual repatriation. These documented workers would be registered with a labor union (thus eliminating any opposition from labor), and sent to sectors in which they would not displace local workers. The immigrant workers would thus be protected from abuses that now result from their illegal status, and the labor force would be strengthened.

Foreign Investment

Foreign investment in Mexico has been discouraged both by the economic crisis and by a lack of communication, which has misled foreign investors regarding relevant Mexican regulations. The 1973 law, in spite of current opinion, did not essentially change the rules of the game; it only brought together certain principles, such as those sectors of the economy that were reserved for the state exclusively and those that were reserved to Mexican citizens only.

The Foreign Investment Law went into effect in 1974. The experience since then demonstrates that when the Mexican economy grows, so does foreign investment, and when the economy declines, foreign investment declines. This proves that the existing law is not a deterrent to foreign investment; rather, the amount of capital invested varies according to the economic situation.

Foreign Debt

Mexico's foreign debt is the result of a process initiated by the international banks. These banks transferred their excess of liquidity to Mexico and other countries in order to benefit from the economic boom taking place in those countries at the time. However, even though both the banks and Mexico itself made mistakes that propagated the foreign debt, until now Mexico alone has coped with the costs of those mistakes. Mexico has made all of the sacrifices, even though these have frequently surpassed morally and socially acceptable limits, while the international banks have continued to increase their profits. The banks shared in the benefits of Mexico's economic boom; furthermore, by providing funds that helped postpone necessary adjustments in the Mexican economy, the banks helped make the present corrections more difficult and expensive than they would otherwise have been. Therefore, elementary justice requires that the banks now share in the costs resulting from the crisis.

A fair solution to the problem would involve reducing interest rates, eliminating financial spreads, and restructuring the total debt to reflect its real value and Mexico's ability to repay it. This plan would solve the debt problem equitably, forcing the two parties to truly share responsibility.[2]

The U.S. Government could substantially contribute to the design of a solution to the debt problem by modifying the pertinent rules and regulations, so that creditor banks could declare part of the debt a "nonperforming asset," without significantly affecting their profits.

Oil

Mexico is the main oil supplier to the United States, providing 20 percent of total U.S. oil imports. For Mexico, too, the oil trade with the United States is vitally important, since oil represents half of total exports. The economic advantages that make Mexico a convenient oil supplier for the United States are undeniable, but there are also strategic considerations. Geographic proximity, the abundance of resources and the certainty of supply make Mexican oil important for the United States. Aside from Mexico, only Canada can supply the United States with oil by land; this factor is particularly valuable during times of crisis. Given these considerations, the U.S. unilateral decision in 1986 to charge a discriminatory tax on the refining of imported crude oil, in violation of the GATT rules and without making an exception for Mexico, is most reprehensible.

Drug Trafficking

Drug trafficking is not a Mexican problem in its origin. It is an American problem—a problem caused by demand, not by supply. Thus, campaigns against production are useless. Unless demand for these products is reduced, decreasing the Mexican supply will lead only to a substitution of products from another source, as has been proved time and time again. Mexico expends a lot of money, effort, and even human lives in the battle against drug production and trafficking, but this alone will not solve the problem. As long as antisocial and corrupt elements in the United States continue to organize the production, finance, purchase, distribution, and consumption of drugs, all of the efforts by the Mexican Government will prove insufficient.

Regional Conflicts

We believe in the rule of law, not in the right of might. We have always adhered to this principle, and this is one reason why we have a relatively small army for a country of our importance. The fact that we lie between several regional areas places us in a high-risk situation, given the probability of conflict within or between these regions.

That is why Mexico believes that the sovereignty of the countries directly involved in regional conflicts should be respected. This attitude is shared by most other Latin American countries. Therefore, in regional matters, to be against Mexico's policy is to be against the position sustained by most of Latin America.

Multilateral Forums

A relatively new problem in the bilateral relationship is American irritability regarding Mexico's votes in multilateral forums. I believe this reaction is the result of an erroneous perception of Mexico's foreign policy. The United States assumes that Mexico's affirmation of an independent foreign policy constitutes aggression directed against the U.S. Government and the American people. This is incorrect. Mexico is, and always has been, proud of its record in the multilateral organizations, where it has constantly acted in accordance with traditional international principles (although in defending these principles, it has sometimes acted against its own interests). However, as I have already mentioned, Mexico and the United States do not always share the same interests or even the same principles; different degrees of development and different histories sometimes result in diverging points of view.

Mexico wants pluralism to be respected in Latin America, as well as in the rest of the world. It also believes in universal and permanent disarmament, and is a promoter and trustee of the Treaty of Tlatelolco on the prohibition of nuclear arms in Latin America. Without doubt, Mexico will continue to adhere to these principles and to defend them.

Consequently, it is logical, and should not surprise the U.S. Government, that Mexico in multilateral forums will vote against any matter that violates these principles, and that it will actively encourage projects, even those not approved of by the United States, that contribute to the achievement of its foreign policy objectives. This behavior should be understood not as a vote against the United States, but simply as a vote in favor of Mexico's history.

Conclusions

In summary, these are the main points that the United States should consider in designing a policy toward Mexico based on mutual respect and acceptance of a geographic proximity that cannot be changed.

1. The United States must acknowledge that the differences in the interests of these two nations derive from different historical experiences and levels of development, and must respect those differing interests.
2. In order to obtain optimal results from a policy toward Mexico, the areas of coincidence, or common interest, should be examined and built upon.
3. The United States must not pressure and, most of all, must not intervene in Mexico's political activity; it should collaborate in efforts to make Mexico a prosperous and stable country, without expecting Mexico to sacrifice its national identity or its independence.
4. Although good personal relations between high government officials are helpful in carrying out fruitful negotiations, they cannot compensate for differences of interest that exist between our two countries.

Relations between Mexico and the United States have been very contradictory. The complexity of this relationship leaves no doubt that there is a great need for a special policy or special relationship founded on mutual understanding and acceptance of our differences; only on these terms can bilateral relations be beneficial to both nations.

Notes

1. During the First World War, the German Foreign Minister, Arthur Zimmerman, sent a telegram offering Mexico the return of Texas, New Mexico, Arizona and California in exchange for an alliance with Germany against the United States. Mexico refused.
2. In April 1983, I presented this idea in a lecture at the Center of Practical Studies for International Negotiations, in Geneva.

Mexico and the United States: The Lost Path

Adolfo Aguilar Zinser

The bilateral relationship between Mexico and the United States has become more conflictual recently. In the past, the key to the special relationship between the two countries was the U.S. recognition that Mexico's political system was the best guarantor of political and social stability. Since 1982, the United States has become less accepting of Mexico's political system. The resulting increase in tension and conflict between the two countries has spilled over into differences they have regarding debt and Central America. On debt, the United States wants structured change in Mexico in return for U.S. support in debt negotiations. Yet the United States seeks only narrow, short-term solutions to the problem. In Central America, Mexico reduced its commitment to change in order to improve its relations with the United States, but to no avail. The United States instead wants Mexico to help find a solution that serves U.S. interests. Bilateral conflict over these issues has exacerbated political struggles within Mexico.

SINCE THE SECOND WORLD WAR, Mexico and the United States, geographically close, but historically and culturally distant, have learned to live in harmony. Their relationship has been based on practical accommodation of their diverse interests and recognition of their mutual political constraints and realities. Tolerance, necessity, and short-term agreements have served as good substitutes for long-lasting trust and sincere friendship.

From the 1940s until recently, this relationship consisted of a sequence of low-key tensions, manageable conflicts, and careful searches for common grounds of coexistence. In recent bilateral exchanges, however, this order has given way to periodic crises, one more explosive than the next. These previously "respectful" and "mature" neighbors are now a burden, a liability, and a national security problem for each other.

A Marriage of Convenience

Franklin Delano Roosevelt's Good Neighbor Policy was, in 1934, the beginning of this order we see crumbling today. Washington's policy of sympathy toward the hemisphere, and particularly toward Mexico, in practice amounted to polite condescension. Nevertheless, during World War II, members of the American establishment, who had formerly adhered to gunboat diplomacy or the carrot-and-stick approach, sought the support and active endorsement of the revolutionary Mexican regime for the Allied cause.

In the postwar period, Mexico and the rest of Latin America experienced "benign neglect" at the hands of the United States. The U.S. Government had eagerly accepted global responsibilities. Thus, Latin neighbors were not a priority—unless, of course, government officials or business executives interpreted the recurrent social turmoil and political upheavals in the region as "communist expansion" or as threats to national security.

During the cold war years of ideological intolerance and well into the 1970s, Mexico enjoyed the fruits of rapid economic expansion and the most stable and well-entrenched political system of the region. Hence, there was no cause for concern in Washington and no need to look for a better deal than the one offered by the nationalistic regime of the era ushered in by the 1910 Mexican Revolution. Many political observers were astonished by the remarkable achievements of Mexico's economy and its political system, organized around the Institutional Revolutionary Party (PRI). Prestigious American scholars advanced the Mexican "miracle" as a model to be followed by other Third World countries.

Mexico's resistance to American influence, its threats to use popular nationalism to retaliate against unsolicited involvement in domestic affairs, its aggressive anti-American rhetoric, and even its frank disagreement with the United States on delicate regional affairs (Guatemala in 1954 and Cuba in 1962) did not cause a showdown.[1] On the contrary, this assertiveness secured international recognition and praise for Mexico, as well as the admiration of many Americans. Although the Mexican Government used nationalism to claim the respect of the United States, Mexicans were always careful not to turn disagreement into confrontation. Usually through discreet channels, Mexican leaders assured their American counterparts that Mexico's basic national interests and its ideas about the world were compatible with those of the United States.

American politicians did not find in Mexico's behavior a real threat or a worthy challenge. Mexico was considered an aligned neighbor, which, because of its idiosyncrasies, did not wish to be viewed as an unconditional ally. Meanwhile, Mexico was guaranteed stability, thanks to its economic growth and its populist "democratic" authoritarianism. Washington could very well take Mexico for granted.

Nonetheless, as decades passed, this absentminded attitude of tolerance on the part of the United States proved to be too narrow a framework for the intense interactions between the American people and the rapidly growing Mexican population. The idea of a special relationship was advanced, and occasionally truly sought, in recognition of the uniqueness, variety, and complexity of the bilateral interchange. The term "interdependence" was adopted to describe the peculiarities of an unbalanced "silent integration" of the two sharply different economies bound together by geography and by the spontaneous, vigorous, and uncontrolled flow of capital and labor across the border.

Although the U.S.–Mexican relationship is unique, it has never been really special. American attention and priorities have always been elsewhere. Moreover, stubborn Mexican nationalism has kept Mexico from a full strategic embrace with the United States. Although the common interests of Mexico and the United States were not sufficient for building a special relationship, they were sufficient for constructing reliable compromises and, in the most difficult situations, for enabling the two countries to agree to disagree. Thus, the postwar terms of engagement between the two countries were fragile, but remarkably stable. All differences notwithstanding, a real partnership existed.

The key to this peculiar relationship was Washington's reluctant, but uncontested, recognition that Mexico's established political system— with all of its nuances, shortcomings, and irrationalities—was the best partner available to its own. Because Washington placed high priority on Mexico's political and social stability, the possibility of a search for another partner was always discarded as too risky. The American power elite settled for the Mexican regime because the regime guaranteed political stability and sustained economic growth. The Mexican regime, in turn, used this historic recognition as proof of its legitimacy. This unwritten pact had a number of effects: It fixed the political boundaries between the two unequal neighbors; assured the autonomy of the Mexican state; guaranteed the Mexican leadership that Washington would comply with established limits on intervention in Mexico's internal affairs; established the boundaries of American economic inroads in Mexico; allowed for much flexibility in Mexican compromises with U.S. interests; created the conditions of mutual confidence and discretion necessary to manage bilateral disagreements; and created an American complicity with the undemocratic practices of the PRI.

The Broken Promises

Since 1982, the unwritten understanding with Mexico has been seriously and openly questioned in the United States. It is now clear that the old order is in serious jeopardy and that no constructive alternative is in the making. Today, Mexico and the United States are portrayed as distant neighbors. Anger, distrust, disappointment, and a sense of insecurity permeate American feelings and opinions—informed and uninformed—about Mexico. In turn, most Mexicans, even many of those who sympathize with the "American way of life," fear the beginning of a grave conflict with the United States. Rancor against the United States and a sense of humiliation have ignited the spirit of Mexicans from all walks of life. Public feelings between Mexicans and Americans are, evidently, on a collision course.

A long history of mutual offenses, real or imagined, has surfaced and is being manifested, with unusual bitterness, in a new and complex set of political problems, ideological trends, and economic events in both countries. No single factor, motivation, or attitude can by itself explain the rapid erosion of U.S.–Mexican relations. It is a general phenomenon, encompassing every bilateral issue and discussion. Dialogue, positive measures, productive contacts among public officials, and instances of cooperation and understanding still exist; however, they are only manifestations of the status quo, with virtually no constructive results.

The majority of American political analysts conclude that the most important source of friction in U.S.–Mexican relations is Mexico itself. The combination of corruption, mismanagement, economic crisis, financial bankruptcy, and loss of political clout and legitimacy is, in the eyes of most American observers, sufficient reason to justify their feelings of apprehension and dismay toward Mexico.

The coincident impatience, hostility, and disapproval of American bureaucracies, institutions, organizations, individuals, and media toward Mexico is most likely not the result of a concerted effort. In spite of attempts by some Reagan administration officials to organize covert operations against Mexico, the antipathy toward Mexico is so widespread, no one individual or organization has the power or skill to be responsible for having launched it. Nonetheless, this active disapproval seems to be inspired by three basic assumptions: First is the perception that the "Mexican way" of doing things and of approaching problems is increasingly wrong, and is determined by corruption, authoritarianism, populism, and irrational nationalism. This view leads to the conclusion that Mexico's political decisions result in inefficiency, public frustration, and cynicism, which, in turn, become the source of possible political unrest and serious problems for the United States. Second, because of the idea that the Mexican way has lost its consistency, strength, and credibility, Americans no longer consider the Mexican government a reliable partner or a convincing interlocutor. Third, there is a view that the Mexican leadership has lost its power to resist pressure and its ability to stop direct American involvement in Mexican affairs. Therefore, in the United States, criticizing the Mexican way, and demanding that the Mexican Government publicly endorse American ideas and reverse its prior positions and commitments, is considered an approach that has no political cost, has no potential for creating a crisis, and brings no danger of retaliation or risk of a backlash.

This widespread perception about the weakness of the Mexican system has fomented rage and antipathy, but it has also encouraged great expectations in the United States. The result has been to enlarge the bilateral agenda to implicitly or explicitly include subjects that were previously considered off-limits. Elections, government corruption, the excesses of presidential power, and public ownership of vital resources are subjects that now have at least as much to do with U.S.–Mexican relations as immigration, trade, fisheries, or the environment. Nothing is forbidden or fixed; everything is negotiable and open to question.

Mexican scholars, commentators, and politicians do not give a coherent and convincing view of what is really causing the collapse of this crucial relationship. Most analysts talk only about the existence of an American "conspiracy" and a "defamatory campaign," and blame the United States for the difficult economic climate and other misfortunes faced by Mexico. However, a large number of Mexicans recognize that it is their country's inability to cope with its problems and to project political leadership, assertiveness, and a sense of direction that places it at the mercy of mounting American criticism and possible intervention. More and more Mexicans share the view that in the absence of true and meaningful democratic reform—that begins, but does not end, with respect for the vote—and without economic reorganization to fill social gaps and gain efficiency and international competitiveness, nationalistic Mexican ideals are worthless. Many Mexican intellectuals, entrepreneurs, young professionals, and political activists strongly reject the implicit PRI contention that to preserve national sovereignty from American ambitions, citizens must tolerate, or even justify, corruption, electoral fraud, and social misery. Neither do they accept the proposition of prominent businessmen and conservative political activists that to surrender to a "benign" American tutelage is a necessary or convenient way to correct Mexico's flaws and modernize and democratize the country.

Discord between Mexico and the United States comes at a time when delicate and pressing issues crowd the bilateral agenda. A brief look at two of the outstanding bilateral problems is sufficient to verify how much the environment has changed for the worse. The debt problem and the conflict in Central America are not the only areas where the lack of mutual understanding precludes constructive U.S.–Mexican interaction. Immigration, drugs, and the border present issues on which the countries are equally at odds. However, it is in the areas of geopolitics and the economy that extreme unilateral action from either side is possible, potentially leading to a serious collision.

Mexico's Debt: A Costly Bill of Political Payments

Since 1982, largely as a consequence of the debt, economic negotiations between Mexico and the United States have gradually moved away from traditional case-by-case discussion of an agreed agenda, toward a new framework unilaterally imposed by Washington: a comprehensive assessment of the overall economic strategies, objectives, and policy instruments of the Mexican Government. Indeed, the subject of bilateral negotiations is no longer limited to specific areas of mutual economic exchange, but is bluntly focused on discussion of Mexico's general economic performance. "Structural change" is the name of the game, which means that to normalize its economic relations with the United States and to get the support of the U.S. Government in crucial debt negotiations, Mexico has to slash protectionism and subsidies, reverse the role of the state in the economy, reorganize its public sector, and relinquish to private business—national and foreign—the leadership role in development.

In contrast to these enormous demands for economic reorganization, Washington has approached the debt problem itself—since the first rescue operation of 1982—very narrowly, by seeking only immediate, short-term solutions. The United States has failed to offer Mexico, or even to consider and discuss with Mexico, any substantial relief. Washington has only offered Mexico credits to meet its immediate financial obligations and new loans to keep its debt rolling, thereby creating an increasingly vicious circle. However, the Reagan adminis-

tration has taken advantage of Mexico's financial bankruptcy and political vulnerability to demand much more than short-term adjustments
to the Mexican economy. In the last round of comprehensive negotiations between Mexico and its creditors (which began in the summer of
1986, and ended early in 1987 with the approval of a 14.5 billion dollar
package of new money for Mexico), the Reagan administration accepted almost no Mexican suggestion. President Miguel de la Madrid's
idea of lowering interest payments and freeing those resources to
finance his recovery program was particularly spurned. The Reagan
administration virtually forced the banks and the International Monetary Fund (IMF) to give new money to pay interest to the commercial
banks and forced Mexico to take it. That was all Mexico got.

In the United States, there are several schools of thought about
Mexico and its debt. One, still in the minority, is that Mexico should not
be bailed out again and that no more relief funds should be given to
Mexico until political and economic conditions there change radically.
According to this theory, no word, promise, or commitment from the
Mexican Government should be accepted by the United States as a
valid guarantee that the right policies will be implemented. Therefore,
the United States should intervene directly, using all of its leverage and
its resources, to secure Mexico's economic and political liberalization.

Others in the Reagan administration champion a more cautious
approach: Keep the Mexican Government on the hook with a steady
line of credit in exchange for more conditions. The purpose is, first and
foremost, to protect the international financial system from a default.
Second, the objective is to monitor with heavy leverage Mexico's performance with respect to structural change. Many conservative Americans still believe that economic orthodoxy and tight credit are the only
way to bring back positive growth rates. They also think that if payment conditions are softened and fresh credit is provided, Mexico will
be led away from orthodox policies and back to heavy public spending
and more state control of the economy.

Some liberals believe that a new approach is necessary. They argue
for a more flexible, heterodox policy to improve the chances for economic growth and liberalization, and they propose a meaningful reduction in interest payments to free resources that can be used effi-
ciently to create jobs, reinforce political stability, and promote
democratic change.

Nevertheless, liberals and conservatives alike do not want the Mexican authorities to choose their economic strategies on their own. Even
the most moderate, generous, and cooperative of all proposals, such as
that of Senator Bill Bradley, strongly recommends the establishment of

a surveillance mechanism—a "council" (although perhaps not the IMF)—to oversee Mexico, as a precondition to granting Mexico significant debt concessions. In short, the moderates argue that Mexican leaders should be persuaded or forced to action in accordance with American tutelage. An autonomous solution by Mexico to its economic problems is unanimously considered unreliable and undesirable.

Whatever approach is taken, a real and unavoidable dilemma exists in Mexico between economic growth and debt servicing. This dilemma will not be resolved unless a major departure from the current conditions of payment is unilaterally imposed by Mexico, agreed to by the United States, and accepted by the creditors through a settlement negotiated outside of the present system. Mexico is trapped, and U.S.–Mexican relations are at an impasse, because there is no political incentive in Washington to work out a cooperative solution with Mexico outside of the existing system. Mexico's credibility is so low that in spite of genuine fears of default among creditors, nobody gives much credence anymore to its sporadic threats to resort to a suspension of payments or to impose unilateral limits on them. Instead, American politicians and most bankers deal with Mexico under the assumption that the Mexican government is more afraid than they are of the political and economic consequences of a moratorium.

A transition to an environment of cooperation is possible only if Mexicans and Americans regain confidence in Mexico's ability to conduct its own affairs. Firmer, more astute, and more effective leadership in Mexico, and recognition in the United States that less direct American involvement in Mexican affairs would reduce conflict between the two countries and increase Mexico's credibility, could lead to such a resurgence of confidence.

Central America: Beyond the Point of No Return

On the bilateral agenda of Mexico and the United States, there has always been a place for the Caribbean and Central America. Under normal circumstances, it is a dormant issue; occasionally, however, in times of crisis, it surfaces as the focus of intense debate. Since the 19th century, American politicians have refused to discard the possibility that their Mexican neighbors might eventually become their rivals. However, a tacit agreement was reached long ago that Mexico would keep out of the political quarrels of its neighbors.

It was in the 1970s, in conjunction with other episodes òf defiance— the collision over the strategic question of oil and natural gas shipments and the refusal of President Jóse López Portillo to readmit the dying

Shah of Iran—that Mexico challenged this agreement and started to play its own power game in Central America. This happened at the same time that the social and political conflict in Central America captured the attention of ideologues and political and military strategists in Washington, and inflamed their imaginations with unprecedented passion and interest for their Central American neighbors. The backyard was suddenly regarded as the most important and immediate opportunity for the United States to protect its national security, defend its vital interests, prove the effectiveness of its military power and might, and reassert its international prestige with allies and foes alike. In such a serious matter, there was no place for the Mexican franchise or for its unsolicited advice.

Today, disagreement over Central America is widely regarded by political analysts on both sides of the border as one of the main causes of trouble between Mexico and the United States. Many Mexicans explain the antagonism of the Reagan administration and the negative coverage Mexico gets in the American press as nothing more than a well-orchestrated plot to suppress Mexico's active and independent foreign policy, especially in Central America. As if to ratify these perceptions, the Reagan administration insists that it is Mexico's multilateral diplomacy and its attitude toward Central America that sour its relationship with the United States.

However, the shaky role Mexico plays today in Central America bears no relation to the rapid erosion of the Mexican–American understanding. The United States keeps a close eye on Mexico's Central American policy, because of what Mexican sympathy for revolutions has meant to the United States in the recent past, and because of American concern with where Mexican loyalties ought to lie in the future. Moreover, many American strategists are convinced that with its capricious attitudes of independence or with its simple refusal to assume what should be the natural role of U.S. ally and friend in the region, Mexico strengthens American enemies and weakens the prestige and credibility of U.S. policies. Thus, the geopolitical aspect of the bilateral relationship has emerged for the first time in recent history as fundamental grounds for a redefinition of the framework and limits of the relationship. At stake are the strategic considerations of the bilateral understanding and the explicit definition of friendship and neighborliness.

Because of the lack of consensus in the United States about the causes of the conflict and about the true importance of Central America for U.S. national security, opinions about the role Mexico should play in Central America have been deeply divided. Many liberal Democrats and intellectuals have regarded the independent position taken by Mexico as a constructive alternative to Reagan's Central American policy. The Mexican Government has deliberately promoted this view by attempting to portray itself as a friend offering its good services; by suggesting another way of protecting the national interests of the United States in the region; by presenting itself as a willing conduit between the United States, and the Sandinistas, Cuba, and the Salvadoran guerrillas; and by guaranteeing with its own word and prestige whatever deal Washington could make with any of the parties involved. However, as the Mexican posture has softened,[2] liberal critics have denounced Mexican inconsistencies. Today, the American Right condemns Mexico for being too leftist in Central America, and the American Left denounces Mexico for being too soft on Reagan's policies in the region.

There is debate in Mexico about the motivations and justifications for active Mexican opposition to U.S. policies in Central America. The key question is how vital Mexican interests are served by those actions. To many, it seems clear now that Lopez Portillo was overly confident about Mexico's oil prestige and that he improvised a leadership role in Central America without thinking of the grave consequences his actions could have on U.S.–Mexican relations. For many Mexicans, support of the Salvadoran revolution, defense of the Sandinista regime, and even participation in the Contadora peace process have posed so many ideological, political, and practical questions and problems that the further Mexico distances itself from those issues, the better.

The de la Madrid administration, for example, was convinced that the irresponsible policies of its predecessor, including the López Portillo administration's conduct in Central America, were to blame for Mexico's trouble with the United States. According to the de la Madrid administration, Mexico could regain American confidence simply by moving away from previous postures on regional affairs and retreating to a neutral distance, keeping the symbolism, but not the substance or the aggressive rhetoric, of previous years. Consequently, the Contadora Group was created in January 1983 to find a compromise with, rather than to battle against, Reagan's policies.

In crossing the line in Central America without a careful assessment of the possible consequences, Mexico placed itself in a dangerous position. However, stepping into the Central American conflict was not a completely irrational or groundless action for Mexico. For the first time in its history, Mexico adopted a foreign policy stance not simply as a question of principle, but as a matter of national interest. In initial exchanges between Mexican and American leaders, the Mexicans stressed that the cause of the revolutionary conflict in the region was not East–West rivalry, but local political and social oppression; thus, change in Nicaragua, El Salvador, or Guatemala was a historical necessity and, consequently, did not pose a threat to the vital national security interests of the United States in the hemisphere. The Mexicans also expressed their overriding concern that within the framework of a violent confrontation in Central America, including direct American military involvement, the U.S. Government would ultimately demand that every country near the war zone declare itself an enemy or a friend of the United States, and would accordingly extort onerous concessions or bestow advantageous rewards. Furthermore, many Mexicans perceived U.S. military escalation as an opportunity for the United States to limit the political independence and to destroy the national aspirations of every country in the area, including Mexico. However, it was also clear to the Mexican Government that change in the region could take place only at the expense of American hegemony over those countries gripped by revolution, and this was obviously perceived as presenting a very favorable historical opportunity for Mexico.

By giving up its political commitment and sympathy for change in Central America, Mexico has not improved its relationship with the United States. On the contrary, the display of Mexican weakness and insecurity has raised U.S. expectations for a change in Mexican policy. In any event, whatever good or bad reasons Mexico had for getting involved, and whatever clever or foolish actions Mexico took, Central America is not an alien cause to Mexico. Like it or not, Mexico has the right to be involved in this regional struggle. The stakes are very high, and the United States has invested so many resources and so much power and prestige in Central America that the outcome will redefine, for better or worse, the basic ground rules of the relationship Washington has with every country in the region.

Although the Mexican government tried to cut its losses, save face, and pull out of Central America, this proved difficult to do. The United States does not want Mexico to be a bystander; it wants Mexico to be a willing partner in finding a solution that will serve U.S. interests. Unilateral Mexican withdrawal is unacceptable to the United States. Conservatives expect no less than a de facto capitulation by Mexico, so that Mexico would join forces with the United States in the diplomatic, economic, and military war against the Sandinistas in Nicaragua and against left-wing insurgents elsewhere. They would consider this proof of the Mexican Government's commitment to a new strategic understanding and friendship with the United States, and a precondition to building a new framework for the relationship. On the other hand, many liberals want Mexico to play a more assertive role in the region, not as a power contender but as a power broker. Most of the support that the Contadora process received in the United States, before peace negotiations moved from the Contadora framework to that of the Arias peace plan, was based on the assumption that Mexico would use its influence to bring about political liberalization in revolutionary Nicaragua and get all parties, especially the Sandinistas, to the negotiating table. Liberals and moderates also wanted the Mexicans to fight against President Reagan's policy and in favor of U.S. support for a diplomatic solution.

Since the Esquipulas II declaration was signed on August 6, 1987 by the five Central American presidents, Contadora has been displaced from the front line of negotiations and Mexican diplomats feel defeated by the internationally acclaimed success of the Costa Rican plan. This has placed Mexico's Central American policy in limbo. Despite gestures such as Mexico's termination of strategic oil supplies to Nicaragua, conservatives continue to view Mexico with great resentment and suspicion. They argue vehemently that Mexico will soon be a paramount national security problem for the United States and the arena of the same kind of ideological struggle that today exists in Nicaragua.

Washington thus presents Mexico with two unacceptable options: One is to actively and vigorously oppose the conservative strategy in the region and the other is to assure Washington that Mexico is in fact its ally in Central America. The latter would require Mexico to pull away from any initiative that the United States opposes or to work with an agenda previously agreed upon with Washington. These are tough choices that the government in Mexico City would obviously like to avoid.

The United States in the Eye of the Mexican Storm

The debt problem and the Central American conflict show how seriously Washington has Mexico on probation and how deeply Washington is challenging the political personality of the current Mexican leadership. To regain the confidence of the American elite and be accepted again as an effective interlocutor, the Mexican leadership must prove itself—first, in its willingness and its ability to transform the economy according to a set of specific international demands, and then, in its commitment to fulfill its basic duties as an American ally. These vague but widespread expectations are an attempt to force on Mexicans a deep conversion that they do not necessarily want or need.

Furthermore, as long as the legitimacy of the Mexican system depends on the government's concessions to Washington, the country will split bitterly on how to deal with the United States. This could reopen historical wounds.

The somber climate of U.S.–Mexican relations has accelerated the political struggle and encouraged ideological allegiances and groupings among bureaucratic, popular, economic, and intellectual elites in Mexico. Impatience with economic stagnation, inflation, and unemployment, as well as public disillusionment with government corruption and inefficiency, electoral fraud, and bureaucracy is gaining momentum. However, none of the issues has yet produced an open confrontation with the state or a clear challenge to established political control.

In contrast to what most observers in the United States believe, the real political struggle in Mexico is not taking place in the electoral arena, and the contenders are not the PRI and the National Action Party (PAN). Electoral politics is a growing issue, but still a sideshow. The big prize is not to replace the PRI and the state structure, but to gain bureaucratic and political control of either one. This means that the most serious proposals for economic modernization and political democratization originate from within, not outside of, the system. It also means they represent the views of elites in the private and public sectors that call not for the destruction of the current system, but for its preservation through significant reforms.

Except for some stubborn and very ambitious top technocrats on the de la Madrid team, everyone knows that the economy, as well as the political system and the country as a whole, has to adjust quickly to the present internal and external circumstances. The basic disagreement has to do with the role the United States will be allowed to play in the reform. All concerned agree that the size of the state must be reduced, but there is no consensus on what criteria should prevail—those imposed by foreign demands, or by domestic needs and circumstances. There is also no consensus on which areas should be closed down or sold out, and when and how to go about it. All parties also agree that Mexico has to find its place in the world economy if it is to rebuild its own economy, but there is disagreement as to how integrated Mexico's economy should become with that of the United States.

Democratization is also not the real issue in dispute: Most Mexicans, including thousands of PRI cadres, think that the electoral monopoly of the official party has to end, and that the only reasonable and nonviolent way to end it is simply to respect the will of the voters. However, Mexicans disagree on how to advance democracy and at the same time preserve national sovereignty (especially in the northern states, where very powerful public and private American interests want to be much more than simply observers of the electoral process); or how to organize democratic options; and on what else to do to build democracy (in labor unions, parties, universities, the media, and so forth).

Finally, the need for social and economic justice is unanimously regarded as a precondition to the maintenance of political and social stability. The debate here is how much of the foreign debt to pay, how to do it, and how to organize the resources and develop the strategies to reconcile efficiency, competitiveness, and growth with the pressing demands of millions of Mexicans for nutrition, employment, education, health, and housing.

With regard to the future role of the United States in Mexico, the debate centers on two issues—how to conduct the economy (particularly, how to pay and manage the debt), and how to divide and redistribute the economic and political assets of the gigantic state. On one side are powerful Mexicans who favor some kind of negotiated and "benign" American tutelage, subscribe to a docile geopolitical alliance with the United States, and dream of an American-style bipartisan democracy for Mexico. Consequently, even though many of them agree that interest payments are killing economic growth, they want to avoid confrontation with Washington and New York over debt payments. They want direct foreign investment to replace a big portion of the current flow of dollar credits to the government, and they expect the large private Mexican monopolies to benefit from less state involvement in the economy. They also want to see managers, charismatic leaders, and technocrats take political and bureaucratic control of the federal and state governments.

On the other end of the spectrum are those who propose canceling or unilaterally reducing debt payments. For them, a smaller state apparatus is desirable if stronger, more independent, and truly uncorrupt labor and peasant unions are allowed to function. They also want significant internal reform of the PRI, so as to promote new democratic leadership and displace bureaucrats and technocrats. They propose that small and medium-sized private firms band together with different kinds of social enterprises (cooperatives and rural peasant industries that are helped, but not controlled, by the state). They believe that none of these measures can be put into effect if Mexico chooses to be a satellite democracy of the United States.

The first group looks for a solid political base among the very large middle classes in urban centers, especially in the north and in Mexico City; the second group is appealing to workers, peasants, youth, the unemployed, and the displaced in urban centers everywhere. Both groups lack strong leadership, but each has many bright, well-educated, and courageous adherents. Neither current advocates violence or the destruction of the constitutional order. Neither wants to surrender total autonomy to the United States. The more nationalistic current knows that a basic accommodation with the United States would have to be worked out, but wants to negotiate it from a position of strength. Both schools favor a strong, modern, powerful, and proud Mexican leadership, not simply an American protectorate. Nevertheless, the price one group is willing to pay in exchange for American recognition of its leadership is obviously much higher than the concessions the other group considers acceptable.

There is also a third group involved in the power struggle. This is where the real statists, the authoritarians, the anti-democratics, and the coup supporters can be found. Contrary to popular American belief, they are not the Marxist–Leninist radicals, who are too naive, too disorganized, too small and too marginal to count, but the far Right, entrenched mostly in the ranks of the state security apparatus and in some frustrated business circles. They also have many followers among religious and anti-communist fanatics, within some sectors of the military, in the ranks of the state bureaucracy, and, potentially, in the middle classes. They are the strongest advocates of U.S. intervention in Mexico. They know their best chance of winning lies not in open political confrontation, but in hiding, and waiting for the opportunity to take control in the midst of chaos. Their access to power will depend on the inability of the PRI to accept reform, the deterioration of the authority and legitimacy of the state, the erosion of public respect for the presidency, and the amount of repression used to overcome potential unrest. Dictatorship is still the choice of few Mexicans, but Mexico may go in that direction, pushed by American impatience and opportunism, American paranoia of left-wing subversion, and the American public's insecurity over the political transition taking place in Mexico.

Notes

1. Mexico was careful to keep its disagreement with the United States on regional affairs at the level of multilateral and legal discussions on the principle of nonintervention. The Mexican Government also found the proper occasions to strongly condemn communism. See: Mario Ojeda Gómez, "Las Relaciones de México con el Regimen Revolucionario Cubano," *Foco Internacional*, 14 (4): 474–506, 1974.

2. Examples of Mexican withdrawal from previous policy positions include the cancellation of the vital oil shipments to Nicaragua in 1985 (Mexico gave financial reasons as the cause), the cold and distant Mexican attitude toward the revolutionary cause in El Salvador, and the docile and friendly attitude toward the Guatemalan border incidents and the question of the refugees. For an early account of this shift, see: Adolfo Aguilar Zinser, "Mis Desacuerdos Con La Política Exterior," *Página Uno*, June 1984. See also: Alan Riding, "Beleaguered Mexico Cedes Role as Central America Power Broker," *New York Times*, October 24.

U.S.–Mexican Relations: Time for Change

Donald Lyman

It is time for a change in U.S. policy toward Mexico. U.S. reliance on lofty goals, followed by an ad hoc approach to problems has produced crisis decision-making but not the consistent policies needed to build a lasting friendly realtionship or to help Mexico solve its problems. Instead, the United States should work with Mexico toward resolving a few specific but important problems, especially in the economic arena. These cooperative efforts should focus on trade and investment, technology transfer, regional trade opportunities, market access and capital markets. This more limited focus, with small successes building momentum, might help avoid future crises in Mexico and in U.S.–Mexican relations.

IT IS TIME FOR change in U.S. policy toward Mexico. During the last ten years, policymakers in Washington have proclaimed lofty goals of an improved bilateral relationship and a stronger Mexico. But they have failed to seek those goals in day-to-day policy and have taken an extemporaneous approach to occasional Mexican crises. These crises have been partly overcome because of substantial assistance from Washington. Nevertheless, fundamental economic and political problems in Mexico remain unresolved, and Mexico's relationship with the United States continues to be uneasy.

Today, despite a sharp improvement in its trade balance and foreign exchange reserves, Mexico's economic and political outlook is not promising. Part of the reserve improvement has been with borrowed money; Mexico's debt has increased, not decreased. Much repatriation of capital has been used for speculation in the Mexican stock market, which precipitously collapsed in late 1987. Some of the growth in the trade surplus has come from a new outward orientation among Mexican industrialists, but much of it has come from a deeply undervalued peso and lack of demand at home. Government spending has been cut, but is still too high, and will probably grow in 1988, an election year, resulting in a worsening of already high inflation. This is not to deny

134

the accomplishments of the de la Madrid administration in taking courageous economic steps by applying austerity and opening the economy, only to say that the job is not yet finished. Mexico does not yet have a strong, competitive economy whose adequate performance in the future is assured. The key steps will be up to Mexico to take. Nevertheless, Mexico's principal trading partner, source of direct investment and loans, the United States, can play an important role.

For the United States to play a constructive role, bilateral relations must first improve. U.S.–Mexican relations are still uneasy. Public rhetoric has moderated in both countries, and some working relationships improved during joint efforts to cope with the crises of the past few years. Nevertheless, there is still considerable bilateral tension over the debt, narcotics, immigration, Central America, and certain trade issues, especially lack of intellectual property protection in Mexico for pharmaceuticals, as well as the threat of protectionist trade legislation in the United States. And there is some resentment in Mexico that help from Washington during past crises was given with too many "strings" attached. Each country shares responsibility for the state of the relationship, but, given the burdens of history, the initiative for change will probably have to come from Washington, not Mexico City.

The Mexican people have borne the burdens of austerity and of inflation relatively quietly. They will probably continue to do so, but their continued support or at least acceptance of the political status quo cannot be taken for granted. Indeed, it is possible that PRI candidate Carlos Salinas de Gortari, who will undoubtedly be elected President in July 1988 since PRI has never lost a Presidential election, will focus initially on building a stronger political base for the government before initiating significant new economic changes. Unfortunately, the high cost of the necessary social measures will increase inflation, possibly creating political unrest.

Disorder in Mexico would have tremendous strategic and economic implications for the United States. Our exports would be cut dramatically; our most secure source of imported oil would be jeopardized; opportunities would arise for Cuban and Soviet mischief on our border; and millions of Mexicans would rapidly cross the border into the southwestern United States, which is ill-equipped to receive them. Serious, but less cataclysmic, economic and political problems in Mexico would still affect us substantially, especially in the areas of trade and migration.

Recently, some observers have called for a comprehensive solution to bilateral problems, cutting across issues, agencies, and sectors. There have been calls for a Marshall Plan for Mexico. Although policymakers in Washington during the last ten years have done too little, those advocates of a Marshall Plan for Mexico suggest doing too much. Relations with Mexico have long been characterized by too much conflict, distrust, and complexity for such ambitious efforts to work.

Carter Administration Policy

Recent history shows us what will not work. The Carter administration developed elaborate institutions to improve ties with Mexico. In 1977, the newly installed administration sought better relations with Mexico, mainly because of its oil wealth. But the administration applied a policy that one participant, Richard Feinberg, described as "globalism," which he defined as relying on "generalized rules for the management of bilateral problems."[1] Globalism ignored the troubled history and unique importance of U.S.–Mexican relations. Adherence to this policy led to insufficient sensitivity to Mexico in U.S. efforts to force large natural gas sales at a favorable price and in proposing immigration reform without first consulting with, or at least notifying, the Mexicans.

The global approach weakened bilateral institutions, which were already unlikely to succeed in managing this difficult relationship. The bilateral Consultative Mechanism, devised in 1977, included working groups to deal with political, social, and financial issues. On the U.S. side, the State Department chaired each group, which led to resistance by other participating agencies. More important, the groups lacked well-defined policy goals or strong leadership, especially when policymakers in Washington chose to deal with most key issues outside the mechanism and within a global framework that gave Mexico no special attention or treatment.

In 1978, partly to remedy these deficiencies, the Carter administration carried out a detailed interagency study. Presidential Review Memorandum 41 (PRM-41) concluded that a "special relationship" was needed, implying that Mexico should be treated with sensitivity because of the importance of access to its oil and gas resources. PRM-41 did not specify what constituted a special relationship or how it would be attained or managed, except to stress the need for greater coordination of U.S. policy toward Mexico.

From the Mexican point of view, a special relationship seemed a mixed blessing. For many Mexicans, with their exquisite sensitivity to history, it seemed to threaten interventionism by Washington, and to bring back memories of Woodrow Wilson and even the U.S.–Mexican War of 1846–1848. For others, it produced resentment, because Washington's sudden interest seemed so closely related to Mexico's discovery of large hydrocarbon reserves—also an emotional issue in Mexico since President Lázaro Cárdenas' nationalization of the foreign oil companies 40 years earlier.

On the other hand, many Mexican leaders wanted their country to be treated with special sensitivity and consideration. For them, a special relationship probably meant the kinds of outward signs of U.S. friendship and cooperation that characterized U.S.–Mexican relations in the Johnson and Kennedy years, with no active, substantive transformation of the relationship raising the possibility or appearance of intervention.

In mid-1979, Carter began implementing the special relationship by announcing the appointment of Robert Krueger, a former Congressman from Texas, as U.S. Coordinator for Mexican Affairs, with the title of Ambassador-at-large. Krueger faced a tremendous challenge. Not only was he charged with improving a relationship that had deteriorated severely during President Carter's ill-fated visit to Mexico in February, but he faced formidable institutional hurdles. Ambassador Krueger worked at the State Department, reporting to the Secretary of State, but his relationship to the Bureau of Inter American Affairs of the State Department, to other federal departments and agencies, and to the White House was not clearly defined. As part of State, he had none of the automatic influence on interagency matters that he would have exercised at the National Security Council (NSC) or at the White House, although his personal political power gave him the potential to win some interagency squabbles. But he had little interest in the brutal infighting necessary to assert his primacy at State, in relations with the new and inexperienced American ambassador, Julian Nava, or with other agencies. And the White House never clarified his role or gave him strong backing.

Krueger did seek to strengthen and improve the Consultative Mechanism. Under his guidance, it grew into nine working groups: trade, tourism, border, environment, migration, energy, industry, law enforcement, and finance. State now shared the chairmanship of most groups with other agencies, an arrangement that helped reduce interagency squabbling.

By early 1980, however, the Carter administration had come to view the Consultative Mechanism principally as a means to eliminate Mexico as an issue in the presidential election of 1980. Senator Edward Kennedy, then the strongest rival to President Carter within the Democratic Party, had begun to criticize Carter's ineptitude in dealing with Mexico. His criticisms were vague, but hit home. Meanwhile, bilateral tensions continued to grow in late 1979 and early 1980—especially when Mexico refused to allow the return of the Shah of Iran after he had undergone surgery in the United States. Nevertheless, U.S. officials could point to the existence of the mechanism's many working groups as a sign of improving relations. But there was little effort to make headway on key bilateral issues—trade, immigration, debt—or to deal with Mexico's deep structural economic problems.

In fact, for officials in Washington, Mexico's steady growth, driven by oil earnings and massive borrowing abroad, had obscured the serious underlying economic problems that would bring about the nation's economic crisis in 1982: high government spending, waste, corruption, an overvalued currency, capital flight, uncompetitive goods, worsening distribution of income, and poor infrastructure.

Meanwhile, the Mexican Government did not seem interested in improving the structure and climate of the bilateral relationship, or in obtaining U.S. help, or in dealing itself with Mexico's fundamental economic problems. Encouraged by Mexico's apparent oil wealth, President Jóse López Portillo and Foreign Secretary Jorge Castañeda tried to turn the focus of Mexican foreign policy away from the United States, toward regional and global issues such as Central America and North–South relations. They also tried to diversify trade, especially in oil, away from the United States.

Mexican leaders liked the Consultative Mechanism, perhaps because it was ineffective. It fragmented bilateral relations and thus made it difficult for the United States to use its leverage on such issues as migration and trade to obtain more oil or improved access to Mexican markets. The Mexicans showed remarkable skill in approaching senior Washington officials individually, dividing and confusing them, thus undermining U.S. leverage. Meanwhile, the Mexican Government sought to use its energy resources as a lever to obtain favorable trade and immigration treatment from Washington. It did not, however, want the United States to be able to link action on these or other issues to a specific increase in oil or gas shipments.

The truly successful efforts at cooperation during this period are still little known or appreciated, but perhaps hold lessons for the future. Joint actions to overcome the massive logistical problems posed by huge grain shipments to Mexico in 1980 succeeded in building enduring relationships at the technical level. Even during this period of poor bilateral relations, the International Boundary and Water Commission (IBWC), founded in 1889, continued to deal successfully with sensitive water problems along the border. The key to the success of such groups as the IBWC was lack of publicity, combined with a focus on resolving specific problems. Close technical cooperation built mutual respect and understanding, at least among the individuals involved.

Ambassador Krueger, a scholar of English literature, used to conclude his speeches by paraphrasing John Donne and saying that "the bell tolled" for U.S.–Mexican relations. It tolled quietly. Within the Consultative Mechanism, some groups met often, and others not at all. Few achieved concrete results. Coordination in Washington improved slightly and the mechanism made progress on a few minor issues involving border crossings and the environment. But the United States still lacked a policy directed toward improving ties with Mexico or dealing with its real problems. Perhaps most important, strong leadership and interest from the White House were lacking. However, the administration did succeed by its own measure, in that it prevented Mexico from becoming an election issue in 1980.

Nevertheless, no strong institutional framework had been created. Most important issues—the 1979 natural gas deal, the Mexican refusal to accept the Shah, the Mexican decision against joining the General Agreement on Tariffs & Trade (GATT), the Ixtoc oil spill, the imposition of a U.S. tuna embargo—were handled outside the Consultative Mechanism, usually acrimoniously.

Reagan Administration Policy

President Ronald Reagan has so far shown a more consistent commitment than his predecessor did to improving relations with Mexico. He has also displayed a certain understanding and chemistry in dealing with Mexican leaders that Carter lacked. He and other officials have consistently and publicly stated that the United States wants a strong, stable, friendly Mexico. The administration provided enormous financial assistance during the debt crisis of 1982, and has provided further assistance on other occasions since. It has also been firm but forthcoming on bilateral trade matters. But it has never developed the institutions or the policies necessary to manage day-to-day relations, much less to change the nature of the relationship or to deal with Mexico's underlying problems.

President Reagan's policy toward Mexico began well, considering its *ad hoc* nature. As president-elect, Reagan spoke of the need for a special relationship with both Canada and Mexico, consisting perhaps of some form of North American economic unity, and he met with President López Portillo on the border. He named as ambassador John Gavin, who had long experience in Mexico, extensive contacts there, and complete fluency in Spanish. In June of 1981, President Reagan invited the entire Mexican cabinet to Camp David to meet with most of its

Washington counterparts. Later that year, the United States decided to buy oil for the Strategic Petroleum Reserve from Mexico, at least partly to firm up the Mexican oil export market at a time when world crude markets were falling. Meanwhile, high officials in Washington sought to settle a few pending trade issues, such as an export subsidy case involving Mexican toy balloons, as favorably toward Mexico as legally possible.

Despite its ambitious goals and this promising beginning, the Reagan administration never created adequate institutions to manage relations with Mexico. At Camp David, officials from both countries agreed to form two bilateral groups: the Binational Commission (BNC), which would have a broad mandate to deal with bilateral issues, and the Joint Commission on Commerce and Trade (JCCT). Officials in Washington wanted to avoid the problems of the Consultative Mechanism. There would be no multiplicity of groups or subgroups; State would chair the BNC; the U.S. Trade Representative (USTR) and the Department of Commerce would chair the JCCT; and there would be a determined effort to deal with important issues within the institutional framework.

These two new groups were no more successful than the Consultative Mechanism had been. The JCCT, formed at the height of the battle between Commerce and the USTR for control of trade policy, did not effectively coordinate U.S. economic policy. Moreover, the Mexicans were uncomfortable with the Commission, perhaps because it seemed to deal with sensitive trade issues in a semipublic forum. They resisted the idea of even having it meet, and by 1986 it had faded away.

The Mexicans at first seemed unenthusiastic about the BNC as well. It was, from the start, relatively poor at coordinating U.S. policy and linking issues; but it was not as fragmented as the Consultative Mechanism, and thus raised at least the possibility of effective linkage. When the United States chose not to link issues within the BNC, however, the Mexicans were more willing to agree to periodic meetings.

Both sides still elected to deal with many important issues outside the formal framework. These included most matters pertaining to Central America. Senior financial officials and Ambassador Gavin worked on debt issues apart from the JCCT or BNC. Almost all of the 1985 negotiations on a bilateral subsidies pact and Mexico's 1986 entrance into the GATT took place outside the JCCT.

With the onset of the debt crisis in August 1982, the administration decided that the risk of default was unacceptable and that a financial package for Mexico must be devised. It included a $1 billion advance payment for oil for the U.S. Strategic Petroleum Reserve, close to $2 billion in credit guarantees for purchases of U.S. agricultural products, a $1.85 billion bridge loan from the Bank of International Settlement, and a 90-day delay in payments to commercial bankers of outstanding Mexican debt payments. This was, however, an *ad hoc* and global solution. Fear of widespread third world default, as much as specific concern for Mexico, shaped U.S. policy.

Even the enormous bailout package did not produce an effort by Washington to deal with the causes of the crisis or to place Mexico on the road to sustained economic growth. When Mexico signed an International Monetary Fund (IMF) "austerity" agreement in November 1982, which led to increased U.S. and multilateral assistance, the IMF targets for Mexican economic performance required resolution of the more obvious problems, such as high government spending, exchange controls, and lack of foreign exchange reserves. But because sharp cuts in government spending were not politically acceptable, it was almost inevitable that the targets would not be met. More fundamental to Mexico's future, IMF pressure to cut imports encouraged the economy to be more closed, although it needed to be more open to resume growth on a stronger foundation.

The 1986 loan package, part of the Baker Initiative, took a more growth-oriented approach toward Mexico and included slightly stronger, but still imprecise, conditionality (requirements for change in the Mexican economy). The infusion of $6 billion in new money has enabled the Mexican economy to resume growth in 1987, but it is possible that, as before, such growth might only conceal Mexico's serious economic problems. Moreover, much of the money will go to interest payments. Probably U.S. Government support for this loan package resulted from the wider Baker Initiative, but Mexico's selection as the first recipient of a Baker Initiative package demonstrated its unique importance for Washington.

In trade policy, the Reagan administration has sought to deal slightly more favorably with Mexico than with its other trading partners. In 1985, it concluded a bilateral subsidies pact, despite much Congressional criticism. This pact contained terms similar to those of the GATT subsidies code and thus was somewhat in harmony with the traditional global, multilateral approach to trade with Mexico. Because it did not require signing of the code, it seemed to give Mexico preferential treatment, although this treatment fell far short of a truly special trading relationship. Most important, however, it moved Mexico closer to the multilateral trading system and was the key step in inducing it, less than 6 months later, to announce it would join the GATT.

The Bilateral Framework Agreement signed in November 1987 is mainly a symbolic step forward. It states some general procedures and

principles for trade and investment, and calls for consultation in some
key areas. It does not, however, liberalize trade or investment as the
U.S.–Canada pact does. The administration did not go beyond preferential treatment to seek mutual special market access or to deal with
Mexico's trade-related problems, especially its industries' lack of competitiveness.

Even after the debt crisis of mid-1982, Central America remained the
number-one issue of concern to Washington in its relations with Mexico, especially after Mexico began to play an active role in the Contadora
process in 1983. To senior officials in Washington, Mexico seemed to be
too supportive of the Sandinistas in Nicaragua and too critical of the
governments of El Salvador and Honduras. The NSC ignored Mexican
issues, except as they actually or potentially related to Central America.
The priorities of the Latin American Bureau of the State Department
matched those of the NSC, although the Bureau resisted NSC staff
efforts to link financial and trade policy toward Mexico to Central
American issues.

Ironically, while most officials in Washington saw Central America
as the most important issue in relations with Mexico, President López
Portillo's successor, Miguel de la Madrid, gave highest priority to
improving Mexico's relationship with the United States. Central America remained an important part of his country's foreign policy, but
obtaining favorable trade agreements and financial assistance from the
United States became his principal foreign policy goal. Given Washington's priorities, this required that Mexico try to prevent the United
States from linking crucial trade and financial issues to the Central
America question. Mexican leaders did not seem to have a firm concep-
tion of what characterized a special relationship with the United States,
beyond assured market access and continued financial assistance, but
President de la Madrid clearly gave more importance than his predecessor to improving ties with Washington.

Mexican leaders probably worried needlessly about linkages in U.S.
policies. There was still little effective policy coordination in Washington. Certainly, Mexico's acceptance of politically difficult IMF targets
and its increased flexibility on trade matters—especially its deciding to
enter the GATT and signing a bilateral subsidies pact—owed something to a wish for continued U.S. help on the debt crisis; there was,
however, no conscious effort by policymakers in Washington to link
these issues, or to develop a cohesive, clear policy toward Mexico.

Ambassador Gavin devised occasional linkages, but found it difficult to obtain agreement from Washington. After he left his post in
Mexico, he said:

Working with Washington on policy issues often took 60 to 70 percent of my time. I believed I had to do this if U.S. policy were to be effective. It was difficult, not only because I was in Mexico City and had no formal mandate to coordinate policy in Washington, but because of the many players involved and their different views. It was not as much a matter of bureaucratic turf fights—in fact, most senior officials were very cooperative—as it was the lack of a coordinating mechanism and of a consensus on priorities. All agreed Mexico was of special importance—but what did that mean in practice? Agricultural sales were important, for example. So was the survival of the world financial system. As a result, linkages and a cohesive policy were hard to develop.[2]

Meanwhile, the most effective cooperative efforts continued to be ones that received the least publicity. The IBWC continued its successful work, although it lost some of its effectiveness when the Mexicans refused to let it deal with the most serious sewage and chemical pollution problems on the border. Implementation of the Strategic Petroleum Reserve deal of 1981 led to technical cooperation that overcame some serious logistical and contractual problems. Bilateral consultations on energy took place with increasing depth and frequency. There were a few other quiet successes between 1981 and late 1985: Mexico played an active role in encouraging Argentina not to default on its debt, and the subsidies pact was negotiated in a much more low-key context than the failed attempt in 1980 to have Mexico enter the GATT.

In late 1985, however, U.S.–Mexican relations began to deteriorate. In September, domestic political tension in Mexico grew, as the opposition National Action Party (PAN) challenged the Institutional Revolutionary Party (PRI) more strongly. Moreover, a sharp decline in oil prices hurt an economy that had been in desperate straits since 1982. In addition, the United States began to realize that American narcotics use was out of control, and that Mexico's eradication and interdiction efforts were failing. The U.S. press and Congress focused on harsh criticism of alleged high-level corruption in Mexico, especially tied to narcotics. Finally, trade issues—particularly U.S. disappointment with Mexico's failure to provide adequate patent protection for U.S. pharmaceutical products—again became a serious irritant, despite Mexico's decision to enter the GATT and initial steps toward trade liberalization.

The Reagan administration lacked adequate policies or institutions to avoid this deterioration of relations, despite a wish on both sides to do so. The BNC proved better suited to annual events of public diplomacy than to dealing with knotty problems. The administration never strongly coordinated relations with Mexico, and officials often spoke with discordant, and sometimes harsh, voices.

Conclusions

Instead of repeating past errors or seeking the unattainable, the United States should work with the Mexicans toward resolving a few specific, but important, Mexican problems, especially in the economic area. This would be very different from continuing the *ad hoc* approach to crises, large and small. Special attention, resources, and flexibility from Washington and Mexico City would ensure the success of the initial steps, building trust and momentum toward more ambitious, but related, efforts. Such micro efforts might not have enough effect, even cumulatively, to avoid or overcome the next crisis; more emergency U.S. assistance might be required. But these micro steps, properly supported by Washington and Mexico City, might help avoid an endless repetition of crises.

There should be a sustained attempt to avoid raising public expectations and to avoid making the mere existence of working groups an accomplishment in itself. There should be little or no publicity until there are concrete results. The IBWC, the Strategic Petroleum Reserve, and bilateral energy consultations have proved that this is probably the means of cooperation most likely to succeed.

Trade and investment seem the most promising, the most necessary, and perhaps the most challenging areas for cooperation. Each country has something to offer the other. The United States, the largest market in the world, can offer Mexico technology, products, and investment. Mexico, with its greater than $100 billion gross domestic product, is a significant market, and it can potentially sell the United States competitive manufactured products, especially components, in certain niches, as well as more traditional agricultural and extractive products. This has already begun to occur in the electronics and automotive sectors. Similarly, for investment and technology transfer, as well as for the provision of goods and services, geography and history logically make the United States Mexico's principal partner. The potential for trade, for technology transfer, and for foreign investment to generate foreign exchange, economic growth, and jobs seems to fit the key economic goals of Mexico's leaders.

On the other hand, economic nationalism has been strong in Mexico. Foreign investment has been extremely controversial. President Cárdenas is still high in the pantheon of Mexican heroes; his nationalization of foreign oil companies is celebrated yearly. And recent trade relations have been plagued by numerous conflicts.

It is because of this troubled history that economic cooperation should start with a narrow focus. Instead of trying to set up a massive assistance plan, or to agree on general and abstract principles to govern trade and investment, both countries should try to develop a special trade and investment relationship in a few selected sectors. The sectors initially chosen should be those in which entrenched economic interests in both countries will be threatened as little as possible, and in which business opportunities are promising. Areas where protectionism is strong—such as footwear and textiles in the United States—should be avoided, with the focus instead on sectors with some history of openness and cooperation, such as electronics or food processing.

Cooperation in these sectors could focus on a number of areas:

1. Trade and investment complementarity, taking political and economic realities into consideration
2. Technology transfer on mutually satisfying terms
3. Regional trade opportunities
4. Increased and even preferential market access

Perhaps the *maquiladora* (in-bond) industry could be utilized to help the competitiveness of the economy as a whole. The industry has grown steadily in its role of assembling mostly imported components for export to the United States (with U.S. duties paid only on the value added in Mexico). Much of the developed expertise is in the electronics and automotive sectors. Opening the Mexican economy to more *maquila* products would surely increase the competitiveness of the economy in related product or component areas.

If implemented properly, this approach could lead to the building of competitive industries in Mexico, while minimizing trade disputes with the United States and political problems in both countries. Cooperation could involve businesses, banks, international financial institutions, universities, "think tanks," and governments at the local, state, and national levels. Success would lead to increased economic activity and exports, and could gradually spread from product to product.

Washington and Mexico City should be willing to do everything possible to make these initial steps succeed by encouraging the best people in both countries to get involved and by lending prestige and a sense of urgency, as well as, when appropriate, government resources, to the job. The effort should ultimately be a private, market-driven one, but it will need U.S. Government help and Mexican Government cooperation to get started successfully.

This policy would be unlikely to work quickly enough to avoid further crises, but it has the potential to achieve a situation where such crises will not be repeated indefinitely. It is thus ambitious in its final goal, but gradual in its application. This approach might be disappointing to those who believe only immediate dramatic action can resolve

Mexico's problems or improve bilateral relations, but it seems the one most likely to succeed. This limited focus, with small successes building momentum, might be the best way to avoid future crises in Mexico and in our bilateral relationship.

Notes

1. Richard Feinberg, "Bureaucratic Organization and United States Policy Toward Mexico," in Susan Kaufman Purcell, ed., *Mexico–United States Relations* (New York: Praeger, 1981), pp. 33–34.
2. John Gavin, personal communication, Nov. 17, 1986.

Selected Bibliography

Bailey, Norman A. and Cohen, Richard. *The Mexican Time Bomb*. [A Twentieth Century Fund Paper] New York: Priority Press, 1987.

Camp¦, Roderic A., ed. *Mexico's Political Stability: The Next Five Years*. Westview Special Studies on Latin America and the Caribbean. Boulder and London: Westview Press, 1986.

Cline, Howard F. *The United States and Mexico*. New York: Atheneum, 1973.

Cornelius, Wayne. *The Political Economy of Mexico under Miguel de la Madrid: The Crisis Deepens, 1985–1986*. Research Report Series, 43. La Jolla: Center for U.S.–Mexican Studies, University of California, San Diego, 1986.

Grayson, George W. *The United States and Mexico, Patterns of Influence*. Studies of Influence in International Relations. New York: Praeger Publishers, 1984.

Hansen, Roger D. *The Politics of Mexican Development*. Baltimore and London: The Johns Hopkins University Press, 1971.

Latell, Brian. "Mexico at the Crossroads: The Many Crises of the Political System." Stanford: The Hoover Institution, Stanford University, June 16, 1986.

Levy, Daniel and Szekely, Gabriel. *Mexico, Paradoxes of Stability and Change*. Westview Profiles, Nations of Contemporary Latin America. Boulder: Westview Press, 1983.

Maxfield, Sylvia and Montoya, Ricardo Anzaldúa. *Government and Private Sector in Contemporary Mexico*. Monograph Series, 20. La Jolla: Center for U.S.–Mexican Studies, University of California, San Diego, 1987.

Newell G., Roberto and Rubio F., Luis. *Mexico's Dilemma: The Political Origins of Economic Crisis*. Westview Special Studies on Latin America and the Caribbean. Boulder and London: Westview Press, 1984.

Purcell, Susan Kaufman, ed. *Mexico–U.S. Relations*. New York: The Academy of Political Science and Praeger, 1981.

Riding, Alan. *Distant Neighbors: Portrait of the Mexicans*. New York: Alfred A. Knopf, 1985.

Ronfeldt, David, ed. *The Modern Mexican Military: A Reassessment*. Monograph Series, 15. La Jolla: Center for U.S.–Mexican Studies, University of California, San Diego, 1984.

Rubio F., Luis and Gil-Diaz, Francisco. *A Mexican Response*. [A Twentieth Century Fund Paper] New York: Priority Press, 1987.

Smith, Peter H. *Labyrinths of Power: Political Recruitment in Twentieth-Century Mexico*. Princeton: Princeton Universtiy Press, 1979.

Vázquez, Josefina Zoraida and Meyer, Lorenzo. *The United States and Mexico*. The United States in the World: Foreign Perspectives. Chicago and London: The University of Chicago Press, 1985.

Appendix I:
Chronology of Events in Mexican History

1810–1821	Wars of Independence from Spain.
1821–1823	Constitutional monarchy under General Agustín de Iturbide, ruling as Emperor Agustín I.
1832–1836	Political scene dominated by General Antonio López de Santa Ana.
1836	Texas wins independence from Mexico.
1845	United States annexes Texas.
1846–1848	Mexican American War. The Treaty of Guadalupe Hidalgo cedes half of Mexico's territory to the United States.
1854–1876	Period in Mexican history known as *La Reforma:* President Benito Juárez and the Liberals, through the Constitution of 1857, diminish the power of privileged groups.
1863–1867	Interlude of foreign rule known as The French Intervention or the *Maximiliano:* Ferdinand Maximilian of Hapsburg takes over in the name of Napoleon III.
1876–1910	*El Porfiriato:* Economic and industrial modernization at the expense of social justice and political liberties under the dictatorship of General Porfirio Díaz. Foreign interests flourish.
1910	*Mexican Revolution, Stage I:* The Anti-Reelectionists, led by Francisco I. Madero, call for an end to the Porfiriato and take up arms to protest fraudulent election results.
1911	*Stage II:* Díaz flees to France, Madero elected President.
1913	*Stage III:* Madero and Vice President Pino Suárez killed, Army chief Victoriano Huerta assumes the Presidency. Huerta's dictatorship becomes the target of revolutionary forces, now in three camps: the urban middle classes and intellectuals led by Venustiano Carranza, the northern ranch workers led by Pancho Villa, and the peasants and rural workers, led by Emiliano Zapata.

1914   U.S. president Woodrow Wilson lands Marines in Veracruz.

1914–1917   *Stage IV:* Huerta resigns, leaving Carranza in power. With U.S. assistance Carranza drives Villa and Zapata from the capital. Villa leads revenge attacks across the U.S. border, prompting retaliation by Brig. Gen. John J. Pershing.

1917   Pershing out of Mexico. New Constitution, still in place today, is approved.

1920–1924   Presidency of General Alvaro Obregón.

1924–1934   Period known as the *Maximato,* named for Plutarco Elias Calles, also known as *El Máximo.* Calles, elected once, then ruled Mexico through puppet governments. He consolidated his control by forming a single national party, the PRN (National Revolutionary Party/*Partido Revolucionario Nacional*)

1934–1940   Presidency of General Lázaro Cárdenas: Birth of the Mexican political system as we know it today. Splitting with the Calles machine, Cárdenas reforms the national party, giving it a new name (Mexican Revolutionary Party/Partido Revolucionario Mexicano/PRM), a broader constituency and a new populist agenda, including land reform.

1938   After Mexican Supreme Court finds in favor of the Petroleum Workers' Union in a suit brought by a major U.S. oil company, Cárdenas expropriates 17 foreign oil companies and nationalizes the petroleum industry, forming PEMEX.

1939   PAN (National Action Party/Partido de Acción Nacional) formed in opposition to populist policies of Cárdenas.

1940–1946   Presidency of General Manuel Avila Camacho: Mexico aids U.S. war effort and develops her nascent industry.

1942   Bracero Program designed to fill labor shortages in the U.S.

1946–1952   Administration of Miguel Alemán, the first non-military president since the Revolution: Major industrial and agricultural programs initiate the "Mexican Miracle" of sustained economic growth. The party is renamed the PRI (Institutional Revolutionary Party/*Partido Revolucionario Institucional*).

1952–1958   Presidency of Adolfo Ruiz Cortines.

1954   Operation Wetback results in the deportation of thousands of undocumented workers from the U.S.

1958–1964   Presidency of Adolfo López Mateos.

1964–1970   Presidency of Gustavo Díaz Ordaz.

1968   Political crisis: student protests coincide with Olympiad; kill-
              ing of protesters at the Plaza of the Three Cultures in the
              Tlatelolco section of the capital.

1970–1976   President Luis Echeverría Alvarez tries to placate younger
              generation, offering positions in the PRI and moving more
              to the left in domestic policy.

1976–1982   Presidency of José López Portillo coincides with the rise and
              fall of the oil boom and a period of easy access to foreign
              capital.

1982   Economic crisis begins in August as oil prices plummet.
              López Portillo nationalizes the banks in September.

1982–1988   Presidency of Miguel de la Madrid Hurtado, who inherits an
              unstable economy and an uncertain political situation. He
              calls for "Moral Renovation" and alternatives to traditional
              statist economic policies.

.1987   Finance Minister Carlos Salinas de Gortari chosen as the
              PRI's presidential candidate for the July 1988 elections.

1988   Salinas challenged by two opposition candidates:
              Cuauhtémoc Cárdenas, split from the PRI and running for
              the PARM (Authentic Party of the Mexican Revolution/*Partido
              Auténtico de la Revolución Mexicana*) and Miguel Clouthier of
              the PAN.

Appendix II:
Study Group on
U.S.–Mexico Relations

February–December, 1986

Bruce Babbitt, *Group Chairman, Governor of Arizona*
Susan Kaufman Purcell, *Group Director; Director, Latin American Project, Council on Foreign Relations*
Patricia Ravalgi, *Rapporteur, Council on Foreign Relations*
Christiana Horton, *Rapporteur for Fifth Meeting, Council on Foreign Relations*

First Meeting: February 25, 1986

Discussion Leaders:
Adolfo Aguilar Zinser, *Centro de Investigaciones y Docencia Económicas*
Jorge Castañeda, Jr., *Carnegie Endowment for International Peace*
Rogelio Ramírez de la O., *Ecanal*
Luis Rubio F., *Instituto de Banca y Finanzas (IBAFIN)*

Second Meeting: April 7, 1986

Discussion Leaders:
F. Javier Alejo, *International Finance Corporation,The World Bank*
Baltazar Ponguta, *Vitro, S.A.*

Third Meeting: June 11, 1986

Discussion Leaders:
Humberto Hernández Haddad, *Senator and Head, Foreign Relations Committee, The Mexican Senate*
Rogelio Sada, *Former President, Vitro, S.A.*
Soledad Loaeza, *Centro de Estudios Internacionales, El Colegio de México*
Jorge Castañeda, Jr., *Carnegie Endowment*

Fourth Meeting: September 10, 1986

Discussion Leaders:
Jorge Bustamante, *CEFNOMEX*
Samuel del Villar, *El Colegio de México*
Manuel García y Griego, *El Colegio de México*

151

Doris Meissner, *Carnegie Endowment for International Peace*
Luis Rubio, *Instituto de Banca y Finanzas*
Robert Pastor, *Carter Center, Emory University*

Fifth Meeting: December 3, 1986
Discussion Leaders:
Donald Lyman, *Manager, External Relations,IBM*
Maria Emilia Farías, *Federal Deputy, Mexico*
José Juan de Olloqui, *General Secretary, Banca Serfin*

Group Members

Robert Bartley, *The Wall Street Journal*
Robert Carswell, *Shearman & Sterling*
Leonel Castillo, *Hispanic International University*
Kenneth Dam, *IBM*
Frank del Olmo, *Los Angeles Times*
Guy F. Erb, *GFE, Ltd.*
Richard Feinberg, *Overseas Development Council*
Richard Fisher, *Brown Bros. Harriman & Company*
Susanne Garment, *The Wall Street Journal*
Bart Gellman, *American Horizons*
David A. Hamburg, *Carnegie Corporation of New York*
Antonia Hernández, *MALDEF*
Christopher Isham, *ABC News*
Robert E. Herzstein, *Arnold & Porter*
George W. Landau, *Americas Society*
Robert Leiken, *Carnegie Endowment for International Peace*
Sol Linowitz, *Coudert Brothers*
Richard Mallery, *Snell & Wilmer*
Guillermo Martínez, *The Miami Herald*
William Miller, *Fletcher School, Tufts University*
Mario Moreno, *MALDEF*
Martha T. Muse, *The Tinker Foundation*
Victor Palmieri, *The Palmieri Company*
Capt. Barry Plott, USN, Military Fellow, *Council on Foreign Relations*
Nicholas Rey, *Merrill Lynch White Weld Capital Markets Group*
William Richardson, *U.S. Congressman, New Mexico*
Rodman Rockefeller, *Pocantico Corporation*
Jon Rosenbaum, *Office of the U.S. Trade Representative*
Nestor Sánchez, *Department of Defense*
Susan L. Segal, *Manufacturers Hanover Trust Company*

Isaac Shapiro, *Milbank Tweed*
Ronald K. Shelp, *Celanese Corporation*
Sally Shelton-Colby, *Bankers Trust Company*
Perry Shenkel, *U.S. Department of State*
Theodore Sorensen, *Paul Weiss Rifkin Wharton & Garrison*
Ernest Stern, *The World Bank*
Alan Stoga, *Kissinger Associates*
Viron P. Vaky, *Carnegie Endowment for International Peace*
Sidney Weintraub, *LBJ School, University of Texas*

West Coast Study Group on U.S. Policy Toward Mexico

October, December, 1986

Edward Hamilton, *Group Co-Chairman, Hamilton, Rabinovitz & Alschuler*
Michael Intriligator, *Group Co-Chairman, University of California, Los Angeles*
Susan Kaufman Purcell, Group Director, *Director; Latin American Project, Council on Foreign Relations*

First Meeting: October 30, 1988, Los Angeles

Discussion Leaders:
Adolfo Aguilar Zinser, *Centro de Investigaciones y Docencia Económicas*
Jorge G.Castañeda, *Carnegie Endowment for International Peace*
Susan Kaufman Purcell, *Council on Foreign Relations*
Luis Rubio, *Instituto de Banca y Finanzas*
Rapporteur for First Meeting:
Brian Self, *University of California, Los Angeles*

Second Meeting: December 9, 1986, Los Angeles

Discussion Leaders:
Guy Erb, *Managing Director, Erb & Madian*
Jorge Pinto, *Minister for Economic Affairs and Deputy Chief of Mission, Embassy of Mexico to the United States*
Gustavo Vega, *El Colegio de México*

GROUP MEMBERS

Jeffrey Bortz, *University of California, Los Angeles*
Robert Buchheim, *Consultant, U.S. Arms Control & Disarmament Agency*
Mark Buchman, *Union Bank*
Howard Edwards, *Atlantic Richfield Company*
Murray Fromsen, *University of Southern California*
Frank Fukuyama, *The Rand Corporation*
Edward González, *University of California, Los Angeles*

James Greene, *O'Melveny & Myers*
Paul Johnson, *Sacks, Tierney & Kasen*
Paul Kreisberg, *Council on Foreign Relations*
Paul Langer, *The Rand Corporation*
Jon P. Lovelace, *Capital Research and Management*
Abraham Lowenthal, *University of Southern California*
Ignacio Lozano, *La Opinión*
John Maguire, *Claremont University Center*
Vilma Martínez, *MALDEF*
William Potter, *University of California, Los Angeles*
Roger Revelle, *University of California, San Diego*
Hans Ries, *University of California, Los Angeles*
David Ronfeldt, *The Rand Corporation*
Eric Schunk, *O'Melveny & Myers*
Richard Sherwood, *O'Melveny and Myers*
Richard E. Sherwood, *O'Melveny & Myers*
Peter Tarnoff, *Council on Foreign Relations*

About the Authors

Adolfo Aguilar Zinser, a Mexican political scientist, is currently a Senior Associate at the Carnegie Endowment for International Peace in Washington, D.C.

Jorge Bustamante is the President of the College of the Northern Border (El Colegio de la Frontera Norte) in Tijuana, Mexico.

Jorge G. Castañeda, Professor of Political Science at the Graduate School of the National Autonomous University of Mexico (UNAM), was an adviser to the Mexican government on Central America and Caribbean Affairs from 1979 to 1982.

Manuel García y Griego is Research Professor at the Center for International Studies, El Colegio de México, in Mexico City. He formerly directed the Mexico–U.S. Program of the Colegio's Center for International Studies.

Soledad Loaeza teaches political science and international relations at El Colegio de México and has written extensively on Mexican domestic politics and foreign policy.

Donald Lyman is presently Manager of External Programs for IBM's Americas Group in North Tarrytown, New York. He was a Foreign Service officer from 1977–1984, serving in Bogota, Colombia, Washington and Mexico City.

Doris M. Meissner is currently a Senior Associate at the Carnegie Endowment for International Peace in Washington, D.C. She has held several key positions within the United States Department of Justice, including Acting Commissioner of the U.S. Immigration and Naturalization Service (INS), Deputy Associate Attorney General, and Executive Director of the Cabinet Committee on Illegal Aliens.

José Juan de Olloqui is the Director General of Banca Serfin and is a Director, currently on leave, of the Central Bank of Mexico. Dr. de Olloqui has served as Mexico's Ambassador to the United States and as Undersecretary at the Ministry of Foreign Affairs. He has also been Mexico's Executive Director at the Inter-American Development Bank and President of Mexico's National Securities and Exchange Commission.

Susan Kaufman Purcell is Senior Fellow and Director of the Latin American Project at the Council on Foreign Relations in New York. She was a member of the Policy Planning Staff, U.S. Department of State, with responsibility for Latin America and the Caribbean (1980–1981). Prior to that, she was a professor of political science at the University of California, Los Angeles (1969–1979).

David Ronfeldt is a member of the senior research staff of the Political Science Department of The RAND Corporation in Santa Monica, California, where his research has focused on U.S.–Latin American security relations.

Luis Rubio F. is Director of IBAFIN, Center for Development Research, an independent think tank in Mexico City devoted to the study and analysis of economic and political policy issues. He is a former Planning Director at Citibank (Mexico).